Almanazor and Almahide by John Dryden

Or, The Conquest of Granada by the Spaniards

A TRAGEDY.

THE FIRST PART.

John Dryden was born on August 9th, 1631 in the village rectory of Aldwincle near Thrapston in Northamptonshire. As a boy Dryden lived in the nearby village of Titchmarsh, Northamptonshire. In 1644 he was sent to Westminster School as a King's Scholar.

Dryden obtained his BA in 1654, graduating top of the list for Trinity College, Cambridge that year.

Returning to London during The Protectorate, Dryden now obtained work with Cromwell's Secretary of State, John Thurloe.

At Cromwell's funeral on 23 November 1658 Dryden was in the company of the Puritan poets John Milton and Andrew Marvell. The setting was to be a sea change in English history. From Republic to Monarchy and from one set of lauded poets to what would soon become the Age of Dryden.

The start began later that year when Dryden published the first of his great poems, Heroic Stanzas (1658), a eulogy on Cromwell's death.

With the Restoration of the Monarchy in 1660 Dryden celebrated in verse with Astraea Redux, an authentic royalist panegyric.

With the re-opening of the theatres after the Puritan ban, Dryden began to also write plays. His first play, The Wild Gallant, appeared in 1663 but was not successful. From 1668 on he was contracted to produce three plays a year for the King's Company, in which he became a shareholder. During the 1660s and '70s, theatrical writing was his main source of income.

In 1667, he published Annus Mirabilis, a lengthy historical poem which described the English defeat of the Dutch naval fleet and the Great Fire of London in 1666. It established him as the pre-eminent poet of his generation, and was crucial in his attaining the posts of Poet Laureate (1668) and then historiographer royal (1670).

This was truly the Age of Dryden, he was the foremost English Literary figure in Poetry, Plays, translations and other forms.

In 1694 he began work on what would be his most ambitious and defining work as translator, The Works of Virgil (1697), which was published by subscription. It was a national event.

John Dryden died on May 12th, 1700, and was initially buried in St. Anne's cemetery in Soho, before being exhumed and reburied in Westminster Abbey ten days later.

Index of Contents

THE CONQUEST OF GRANADA. AN INRRODUCTION

This play,—for the two parts only constitute an entire drama betwixt them,—seems to have been a favourite with Dryden, as well as with the public. In the Essay upon Heroic Plays, as well as in the dedication, the character of Almanzor is dwelt upon with that degree of complacency which an author experiences in analyzing a successful effort of his genius. Unquestionably the gross improbability of a hero, by his single arm, turning the tide of battle as he lists, did not appear so shocking in the age of Dryden, as in ours. There is no doubt, that, while personal strength and prowess were of more consequence than military skill and conduct, the feats of a single man were sometimes sufficient to determine the fate of an engagement, more especially when exerted by a knight, sheathed in complete mail, against the heartless and half-armed mass, which constituted the feudal infantry. Those, who have perused Barbour's History of Robert Bruce, Geoffrey de Vinsauf's account of the wars of Richard Coeur de Lion, or even the battles detailed by Froissart and Joinville, are familiar with instances of breaches defended, and battles decided, by the prowess of a single arm. The leader of a feudal army was expected by his followers not only to point out the path to victory but to lead the way in person. It is true, that the military art had been changed in this particular long before the days of Dryden. Complete armour was generally laid aside; fire-arms had superseded the use of the lance and battle-axe; and, above all, the universal institution of standing armies had given discipline and military skill their natural and decisive superiority over untaught strength, and enthusiastic valour. But the memory of what had been, was still familiar to the popular mind, and preserved not only by numerous legends and traditions, but also by the cast of the fashionable works of fiction. It is, indeed, curious to remark, how many minute remnants of a system of ancient manners can be traced long after it has become totally obsolete. Even down to the eighteenth century, the portrait of every soldier of rank was attired in complete armour, though, perhaps, he never saw a suit of mail excepting in the Tower of London; and on the same principle of prescriptive custom, Addison was the first poet who ventured to celebrate a victorious general for skill and conduct, instead of such feats as are appropriated to Guy of Warwick, or Bevis of Hampton. The fashion of attributing mighty effects to individual valour being thus prevalent, even in circumstances when every one knew the supposition to be entirely gratuitous, the same principle, with much greater propriety, continued to be applied in works of fiction, where the scene was usually carried back to times in which the personal strength of a champion really had some efficacy. It must be owned, however, that the authors of the French romances carried the influence of individual strength and courage beyond all bounds of modesty and reason. In the Grand Cyrus, Artamenes, upon a moderate computation, exterminates with his own hand, in the course of the work, at least a hundred thousand fighting men. These monstrous fictions, however, constituted the amusement of the young and the gay[1], in the age of Charles II., and from one of these very books Dryden admits his having drawn, at least in part, the character of his Moorish warrior. The public was, therefore, every way familiarised with such chivalrous exploits as those of Almanzor; and if they did not altogether command the belief, at least they did not revolt the imagination, of an audience: And this must certainly be admitted as a fair apology for the extravagance of his heroic achievements.

But, it is not only the actual effects of Almanzor's valour, which appear to us unnatural, but also the extraordinary principles and motives by which those exertions are guided. Here also, we must look back to the Gothic romances, and to those of Scudery and Calprenede. In fact, the extravagance of sentiment is no less necessary than the extravagance of achievement to constitute a true knight errant; and such is Almanzor. Honour and love were the sole deities worshipped by this extraordinary race, who, though their memory and manners are preserved chiefly in works of fiction, did once exist in real life, and actually conducted armies, and governed kingdoms, upon principles as strained and hyperbolical as those of the Moorish champion. If Almanzor, at the command of his mistress, aids his hated rival to the destruction of his own hopes, he only discharges the duty of a good knight, who was bound to sacrifice himself, and all his hopes and wishes, at the slightest command of her, to whom he had vowed his service, and who, in the language of chivalry, was to him as the soul is to the body. The reader may recollect the memorable invasion of England by James IV. of Scotland, in which he hazarded and actually lost his own life, and the flower of his nobility, because the queen of France, who called him her knight, had commanded him to march three miles on English ground for her sake.

Less can be said to justify the extravagant language in which Almanzor threatens his enemies, and vaunts his own importance. This is not common in the heroes of romance, who are usually as remarkable for their modesty of language as for their prowess; and still more seldom does, in real life, a vain-glorious boaster vindicate by his actions the threats of his tongue. It is true, that men of a fervent and glowing character are apt to strain their speech beyond the modesty of ordinary conversation, and display, in their language, the fire which glows in their bosoms; but the subject of their effusions is usually connected not with their own personal qualities, or feats, but with some extraneous object of their pursuit, or admiration. Thus, the burst of Hotspur concerning the pursuit of honour paints his enthusiastic character; but it would be hard to point out a passage indicating that exuberant confidence in his own prowess, and contempt of every one else, so liberally exhibited by Almanzor. Instances of this defect are but too thickly sown through the piece; for example the following rant.

If from thy hands alone my death can be,
I am immortal, and a God to thee.
If I would kill thee now, thy fate's so low,
That I must stoop ere I can give the blow.
But mine is fixed so far above thy crown,
That all thy men,
Piled on thy back, can never pull it down.
But, at my ease, thy destiny I send,
By ceasing from this hour to be thy friend.
Like heaven, I need but only to stand still;
And, not concurring to thy life, I kill.
Thou canst no title to my duty bring;
I am not thy subject, and my soul's thy king.
Farewell! When I am gone,
There's not a star of thine dare stay with thee:
I'll whistle thy tame fortune after me;
And whirl fate with me wheresoe'er I fly,
As winds drive storms before them in the sky.

This curious passage did not escape the malicious criticism of Settle, who, besides noticing the extravagant egotism of the hero, questions, with some probability, whether Abdalla would have chosen to scale Almanzor's fate, at the risque of the personal consequences of having all his men piled on his own back. In the same scene, Almanzor is so unreasonable as to tell his rival,

—Thou shalt not dare
To be so impudent as to despair.

And again,

What are ten thousand subjects, such as they?
If I am scorned, I'll take myself away.

Dryden's apology for these extravagancies seems to be, that Almanzor is in a passion. But, although talking nonsense is a common effect of passion, it seems hardly one of those consequences adapted to shew forth the character of a hero in theatrical representation.

It must be owned, however, that although the part of Almanzor contains these and other bombastic passages, there are many also which convey what the poet desired to represent—the aspirations of a mind so heroic as almost to surmount the bonds of society and even the very laws of the universe, leaving us often in doubt whether the vehemence of the wish does not even disguise the impossibility of its accomplishment.

Good heaven! thy book of fate before me lay,
But to tear out the journal of this day.
Or, if the order of the world below
Will not the gap of one whole day allow,
Give me that minute when she made her vow.
That minute, even the happy from their bliss might give,

And those, who live in grief, a shorter time would live.
So small a link, if broke, the eternal chain
Would, like divided waters, join again.
It wonnot be; the fugitive is gone,
Pressed by the crowd of following minutes on:
That precious moment's out of nature fled,
And in the heap of common rubbish laid,
Of things that once have been, and now decayed.

In the less inflated parts, the ideas are usually as just, as ingenious and beautiful; for example.

No; there is a necessity in fate.
Why still the brave bold man is fortunate;
He keeps his object ever full in sight,
And that assurance holds him firm and right.
True, 'tis a narrow path that leads to bliss,
But right before there is no precipice;
Fear makes men look aside, and then their footing miss.

The character of Almanzor is well known as the original of Drawcansir, in "The Rehearsal," into whose mouth parodies of some of Dryden's most extravagant flights have been put by the duke of Buckingham. Shaftesbury also, whose family had smarted under Dryden's satire, attempts to trace the applause bestowed on the "Conquest of Granada" to what he calls "the correspondence and relation between our Royal Theatre and popular Circus, or Bear-Garden. For, in the former of these assemblys, 'tis undeniable that, at least, the two upper regions, or galleries, contain such spectators as indifferently frequent each place of sport. So that 'tis no wonder we hear such applause resounded on the victories of an Almanzor, when the same parties had possibly no later than the day before bestowed their applause as freely on the victorious Butcher, the hero of another stage." Miscellaneous Reflections. Miscell. 5.

The other personages of the drama sink into Lilliputians, beside the gigantic Almanzor, although the under plot of the loves of Ozmyn and Benzayda is beautiful in itself, and ingeniously managed. The virtuous Almahide is a fit object for the adoration of Almanzor; but her husband is a poor pageant of royalty. As for Lyndaraxa, her repeated and unparalleled treachery can only be justified by the extreme imbecility of her lovers.

The plot of the play is, in part, taken from history. During the last years of its existence, Granada, the poor remnant of the Moorish empire in Spain, was torn to pieces with intestine discord, and assailed without by the sword of the Christians. The history of the civil wars of Granada, affirmed to be translated into Spanish from the Arabian, gives a romantic, but not altogether fabulous account of their discord. But a romance in the French taste, called Almahide, seems to have been the chief source from which our author drew his plot.

In the conduct of the story there is much brilliancy of event. The reader, or spectator, is never allowed to repose on the scene before him; and although the changes of fortune are too rapid to be either probable, or altogether pleasing, yet they arrest the attention by their splendour and importance, and interest us in spite of our more sober judgment. The introduction of the ghost of Almanzor's mother seems to have been intended to shew how the hero could support even an interview with an inhabitant of the other world. At least, the professed purpose of her coming might have been safely trusted to the virtue of Almahide, and her power over her lover. It afforded an opportunity, however, to throw in some fine poetry, of which Dryden has not failed to avail himself. Were it not a peculiar attribute of the heroic drama, it might be mentioned as a defect, that during the siege of the last possession of the Spanish Moors, by an enemy hated for his religion, and for his success, the principle of patriotism is hardly once alluded to through the whole piece. The fate, or the wishes, of Almahide, Lyndaraxa, and Benzayda, are all that interest the Moorish warriors around them, as if the Christian was not thundering at their gates, to exterminate at once their nation and religion. Indeed, so essentially necessary are the encouragements of beauty to military achievement, that we find queen Isabella ordering to the field of battle a corps de reserve of her maids of honour to animate the fighting warriors with their smiles, and counteract the powerful charms of the Moorish damsels. Nor is it an inferior fault, that, although the characters are called Moors, there is scarce any expression, or allusion, which can fix the reader's attention upon their locality, except an occasional interjection to Alha, or Mahomet.

If, however, the reader can abstract his mind from the qualities now deemed essential to a play, and consider the Conquest of Granada as a piece of romantic poetry, there are few compositions in the English language, which convey a more lively and favourable display of the magnificence of fable, of language, and of action, proper to that style of composition. Amid the splendid ornaments of the structure we lose sight of occasional disproportion and incongruity; and, at an early age particularly, there are few poems which make a more deep impression upon the imagination, than the Conquest of Granada.

The two parts of this drama were brought out in the same season, probably in winter, 1669, or spring, 1670. They were received with such applause, that Langbaine conceives their success to have been the occasion of Dryden's undervaluing his predecessors in dramatic writing. The Conquest of Granada was not printed till 1672.

Footnote

1. There is something ludicrous in the idea of a beauty, or a gallant, of that gay and licentious court poring over a work of five or six folio volumes by way of amusement; but such was the taste of the age, that Fynes Morison, in his precepts to travellers, can "think no book better for his pupils' discourse than Amadis of Gaule; for the knights errant and the ladies of court do therein exchange courtly speeches."

TO HIS ROYAL HIGHNESS THE DUKE[1].

SIR,

Heroic poesy has always been sacred to princes, and to heroes. Thus Virgil inscribed his Æneids to Augustus Cæsar; and of latter ages, Tasso and Ariosto dedicated their poems to the house of Este. It is indeed but justice, that the most excellent and most profitable kind of writing should be addressed by poets to such persons, whose characters have, for the most part, been the guides and patterns of their imitation; and poets, while they imitate, instruct. The feigned hero inflames the true; and the dead virtue animates the living. Since, therefore, the world is governed by precept and example, and both these can only have influence from those persons who are above us; that kind of poesy, which excites to virtue the greatest men, is of the greatest use to human kind.

It is from this consideration, that I have presumed to dedicate to your royal highness these faint representations of your own worth and valour in heroick poetry: Or, to speak more properly, not to dedicate, but to restore to you those ideas, which in the more perfect part of my characters I have taken from you. Heroes may lawfully be delighted with their own praises, both as they are farther incitements to their virtue, and as they are the highest returns which mankind can make them for it.

And certainly, if ever nation were obliged, either by the conduct, the personal[2] valour, or the good fortune of a leader, the English are acknowledging, in all of them, to your royal highness. Your whole life has been a continued series of heroick actions; which you began so early, that you were no sooner named in the world, but it was with praise and admiration. Even the first blossoms of your youth paid us all that could be expected from a ripening manhood. While you practised but the rudiments of war, you out-went all other captains; and have since found none to surpass, but yourself alone. The opening of your glory was like that of light: You shone to us from afar; and disclosed your first beams on distant nations: Yet so, that the lustre of them was spread abroad, and reflected brightly on your native country. You were then an honour to it, when it was a reproach to itself. When the fortunate usurper sent his arms to Flanders, many of the adverse party were vanquished by your fame, ere they tried your valour.[3] The report of it drew over to your ensigns whole troops and companies of converted rebels, and made them forsake successful wickedness, to follow an oppressed and exiled virtue. Your reputation waged war with the enemies of your royal family, even within their trenches; and the more obstinate, or more guilty of them, were forced to be spies over those whom they commanded, lest the name of York should disband that army, in whose fate it was to defeat the Spaniards, and force Dunkirk to surrender. Yet, those victorious forces of the rebels were not able to sustain your arms. Where you charged in person you were a conqueror. It is true, they afterwards recovered courage; and wrested that victory from others which they had lost to you; and it was a greater action for them to rally, than it was to overcome. Thus, by the presence of your royal highness, the English on both sides remained victorious and that army, which was broken by your valour, became a terror to those for whom they conquered. Then it was, that at the cost of other nations you informed and cultivated that valour, which was to defend your native country, and to vindicate its honour from the insolence of our encroaching neighbours. When the Hollanders, not contented to withdraw themselves from the obedience which they owed their lawful sovereign, affronted those by whose charity they were first protected; and, being swelled up to a pre-eminence of trade, by a supine negligence on our side, and a sordid parsimony on their own, dared to dispute the sovereignty of the seas, the eyes of three nations were then cast upon you; and by the joint suffrage of king and people, you were chosen to revenge their common injuries; to which, though you had an undoubted title by your birth, you had a greater by your courage. Neither did the success deceive our hopes and expectations: The most glorious victory which was gained by our navy in that war, was in the first engagement; wherein, even by the confession of our enemies, who ever palliate their own losses, and diminish our advantages, your absolute triumph was acknowledged: You conquered at the Hague, as entirely as at London; and the return of a shattered fleet, without an admiral, left not the most impudent among them the least pretence for a false bonfire, or a dissembled day of public thanksgiving. All our achievements against them afterwards, though we sometimes conquered, and were never overcome, were but a copy of that victory, and they still fell short of their original: somewhat of fortune was ever wanting, to fill up the title of so absolute a defeat; or perhaps the guardian angel of our nation was not enough concerned when you were absent, and would not employ his utmost vigour for a less important stake, than the life and honour of a royal admiral.

And if, since that memorable day,[4] you have had leisure to enjoy in peace the fruits of so glorious a reputation; it was occasion only has been wanting to your courage, for that can never be wanting to occasion. The same ardour still incites you to heroick actions, and the same concernment for all the interests of your king and brother continues to give you restless nights, and a generous emulation for your own glory. You are still meditating on new labours for yourself, and new triumphs for the nation; and when our former enemies again provoke us, you will again solicit fate to provide you another navy to overcome, and another admiral to be slain. You will then lead forth a nation eager to revenge their past injuries; and, like the Romans, inexorable to peace, till they have fully vanquished. Let our enemies make their boast of a surprise,[5] as the Samnities did of a successful stratagem; but the Furcæ Caudinæ will never be forgiven till they are revenged. I have always observed in your royal highness an extreme concernment for the honour of your country; it is a passion common to you with a brother, the most excellent of kings; and in your two persons are eminent the characters which Homer has given us of heroick virtue; the commanding part in Agamemnon, and the executive in Achilles. And I doubt not from both your actions, but to have abundant matter to fill the annals of a glorious reign, and to perform the part of a just historian to my royal master, without intermixing with it any thing of the poet.

In the mean time, while your royal highness is preparing fresh employments for our pens, I have been examining my own forces, and making trial of myself, how I shall be able to transmit you to posterity. I have formed a hero, I confess, not absolutely perfect, but of an excessive and over-boiling courage; but Homer and Tasso are my precedents. Both the Greek and the Italian poet had well considered, that a tame hero, who never transgresses the bounds of moral virtue, would shine but dimly in an epic poem; the strictness of those rules might well give precepts to the reader, but would administer little of occasion to the writer. But a character of an eccentrick virtue is the more exact image of human life, because he is not wholly exempted from its frailties; such a person is Almanzor, whom I present, with all humility, to the patronage of your royal highness. I designed in him a roughness of character, impatient of injuries, and a confidence of himself, almost approaching to an arrogance. But these errors are incident only to great spirits; they are moles and dimples, which hinder not a face from being beautiful, though that beauty be not regular; they are of the number of those amiable imperfections which we see in mistresses, and which we pass over without a strict examination, when they are accompanied with greater graces. And such in Almanzor are a frank and noble openness of nature, an easiness to forgive his conquered enemies, and to protect them in distress; and, above all, an inviolable faith in his affection.

This, sir, I have briefly shadowed to your royal highness, that you may not be ashamed of that hero, whose protection you undertake. Neither would I dedicate him to so illustrious a name, if I were conscious to myself that he did or said any thing which was wholly unworthy of it. However, since it is not just that your royal highness should defend or own what possibly may be my error, I bring before you this accused Almanzor in the nature of a suspected criminal. By the suffrage of the most and best he already is acquitted; and by the sentence of some, condemned. But as I have no reason to stand to the award of my enemies, so neither dare I trust the partiality of my friends: I make my last appeal to your royal highness, as to a sovereign tribunal. Heroes should only be judged by heroes; because they only are capable of measuring great and heroick actions by the rule and standard of their own. If Almanzor has failed in any point of honour, I must therein acknowledge that he deviates from your royal highness, who are the pattern of it. But if at any time he fulfils the parts of personal valour, and of conduct, of a soldier, and of a general; or, if I could yet give him a character more advantageous than what he has, of the most unshaken friend, the greatest of subjects, and the best of masters, I should then draw to all the world a true resemblance of your worth and virtues; at least, as far as they are capable of being copied by the mean abilities of,

SIR,

Your royal highness's
Most humble, and
Most obedient servant,
JOHN DRYDEN.

Footnotes

1. James Duke of York, afterwards James II.

2. Although the valour of the unfortunate James II. seems to have sunk with his good fortune, there is no reason to question his having merited the compliment in the text. The Duke of Buckingham, in his memoirs, has borne witness to the intrepidity with which he encountered the dangers of his desperate naval actions with the Dutch. Captain Carlton, who was also an eye-witness of his deportment on that occasion, says, that while the balls were flying thickly around, the Duke of York was wont to rub his hands, and exclaim chearfully to his captain, "Spragge, Spragge, they follow us fast."

3. When General Lockhart commanded the troops of the Protector in Flanders, the Duke of York was a volunteer in the Spanish army, and was present at the defeat, which the latter received before Dunkirk, 17th of June, 1658.

4. The defeat of the Dutch off Harwich, 3d June, 1665, in which their Admiral, Obdam, was blown up, eighteen of their ships taken, and fourteen destroyed.

5. The author seems to refer to the burning of the English ships at Chatham, by the Dutch Admiral De Ruyter.

ON MR DRYDEN'S PLAY, THE CONQUEST OF GRANADA.

The applause I gave among the foolish crowd
Was not distinguished, though I clapped aloud:
Or, if it had, my judgment had been hid:
I clapped for company, as others did.
Thence may be told the fortune of your play;
Its goodness must be tried another way.
Let's judge it then, and, if we've any skill,
Commend what's good, though we commend it ill.
There will be praise enough; yet not so much,
As if the world had never any such:
Ben Johnson, Beaumont, Fletcher, Shakespeare, are,
As well as you, to have a poet's share.
You, who write after, have, besides, this curse,
You must write better, or you else write worse.
To equal only what was writ before,
Seems stolen, or borrowed from the former store.

Though blind as Homer all the ancients be,
'Tis on their shoulders, like the lame, we see.
Then not to flatter th' age, nor flatter you,
(Praises, though less, are greater when they're true,)
You're equal to the best, out-done by you;
Who had out-done themselves, had they lived now.

VAUGHAN[1].

Footnote

1. John, Lord Vaughan, eldest surviving son of Richard, Earl of Carbery.

DRAMATIS PERSONÆ

MAHOMET BOABDELIN, the last king of Granada.
Prince ABDALLA, his brother.
ABDELMELECH, chief of the Abencerrages.
ZULEMA, chief of the Zegrys.
ABENAMAR, an old Abencerrago.
SELIN, an old Zegry.
OZMYN, a brave young Abencerrago, son to Abenamar.
HAMET, brother to Zulema, a Zegry.
GOMEL, a Zegry.
ALMANZOR.
FERDINAND, king of Spain.
Duke of ARCOS, his General.
Don ALONZO D'AGUILAR, a Spanish Captain.

ALMAHIDE, Queen of Granada.
LYNDARAXA, Sister of ZULEMA, a Zegry Lady.
BENZAYDA, Daughter to SELIN.
ESPERANZA, Slave to the Queen.
HALYMA, Slave to LYNDARAXA.
ISABELLA, Queen of Spain.

Messengers, Guards, Attendants, Men, and Women.

SCENE—Granada, and the Christian Camp besieging it.

PROLOGUE TO THE FIRST PART,

IN A BROAD-BRIMMED HAT, AND WAIST-BELT.[1]

This jest was first of the other house's making,
And, five times tried, has never failed of taking;
For 'twere a shame a poet should be killed
Under the shelter of so broad a shield.
This is that hat, whose very sight did win ye
To laugh and clap as though the devil were in ye.
As then, for Nokes, so now I hope you'll be
So dull, to laugh once more for love of me.
I'll write a play, says one, for I have got
A broad-brimmed hat, and waist-belt, towards a plot.
Says the other, I have one more large than that.
Thus they out-write each other—with a hat!
The brims still grew with every play they writ;
And grew so large, they covered all the wit.
Hat was the play; 'twas language, wit, and tale:
Like them that find meat, drink, and cloth in ale.
What dulness do these mongrel wits confess,
When all their hope is acting of a dress!
Thus, two the best comedians of the age
Must be worn out, with being blocks o' the stage;
Like a young girl, who better things has known,
Beneath their poet's impotence they groan.
See now what charity it was to save!
They thought you liked, what only you forgave;
And brought you more dull sense, dull sense much worse
Than brisk gay nonsense, and the heavier curse.
They bring old iron, and glass upon the stage,
To barter with the Indians of our age.
Still they write on, and like great authors show;
But 'tis as rollers in wet gardens grow
Heavy with dirt, and gathering as they go.
May none, who have so little understood,
To like such trash, presume to praise what's good!
And may those drudges of the stage, whose fate
Is damned dull farce more dully to translate,
Fall under that excise the state thinks fit
To set on all French wares, whose worst is wit.
French farce, worn out at home, is sent abroad;
And, patched up here, is made our English mode.
Henceforth, let poets, ere allowed to write,
Be searched, like duelists before they fight,
For wheel-broad hats, dull honour, all that chaff,
Which makes you mourn, and makes the vulgar laugh:
For these, in plays, are as unlawful arms,

As, in a combat, coats of mail, and charms.

Footnote

1. There is a vague tradition, that, in this grotesque dress, (for the brims of the hat were as broad as a cart-wheel,) Nell Gwyn had the good fortune first to attract the attention of her royal lover. Where the jest lay, is difficult to discover: it seems to have originated with the duke of York's players.

ALMANZOR AND ALMAHIDE

or, THE CONQUEST OF GRANADA.

THE FIRST PART.

ACT I

SCENE I

Enter **BOABDELIN, ABENAMAR, ABDELMELECH**, and **GUARDS**.

BOABDELIN
Thus, in the triumphs of soft peace, I reign;
And, from my walls, defy the powers of Spain;
With pomp and sports my love I celebrate,
While they keep distance, and attend my state.—
Parent to her, whose eyes my soul enthral, [To **ABENAMAR**
Whom I, in hope, already father call,
Abenamar, thy youth these sports has known,
Of which thy age is now spectator grown;
Judge-like thou sit'st, to praise, or to arraign
The flying skirmish of the darted cane:
But, when fierce bulls run loose upon the place,
And our bold Moors their loves with danger grace,
Then heat new-bends thy slacken'd nerves again,
And a short youth runs warm through every vein.

ABENAMAR
I must confess the encounters of this day
Warmed me indeed, but quite another way,—
Not with the fire of youth; but generous rage,
To see the glories of my youthful age
So far out-done.

ABDELMELECH
Castile could never boast, in all its pride;

A pomp so splendid, when the lists, set wide,
Gave room to the fierce bulls, which wildly ran
In Sierra Ronda, ere the war began;
Who, with high nostrils snuffing up the wind,
Now stood the champion of the savage kind.
Just opposite, within the circled place,
Ten of our bold Abencerrages race
(Each brandishing his bull-spear in his hand,)
Did their proud jennets gracefully command.
On their steel'd heads their demi-lances wore
Small pennons, which their ladies' colours bore.
Before this troop did warlike Ozmyn go;
Each lady, as he rode, saluting low;
At the chief stands, with reverence more profound,
His well-taught courser, kneeling, touched the ground;
Thence raised, he sidelong bore his rider on,
Still facing, till he out of sight was gone.

BOABDELIN
You praise him like a friend; and I confess,
His brave deportment merited no less.

ABDELMELECH
Nine bulls were launched by his victorious arm,
Whose wary jennet, shunning still the harm,
Seemed to attend the shock, and then leaped wide:
Mean while, his dext'rous rider, when he spied
The beast just stooping, 'twixt the neck and head
His lance, with never-erring fury, sped.

ABENAMAR
My son did well, and so did Hamet too;
Yet did no more than we were wont to do;
But what the stranger did was more than man.

ABDELMELECH
He finished all those triumphs we began.
One bull, with curled black head, beyond the rest,
And dew-laps hanging from his brawny chest,
With nodding front a while did daring stand,
And with his jetty hoof spurned back the sand;
Then, leaping forth, he bellowed out aloud:
The amazed assistants back each other crowd,
While monarch-like he ranged the listed field;
Some tossed, some gored, some trampling down he killed.
The ignobler Moors from far his rage provoke
With woods of darts, which from his sides he shook.
Mean time your valiant son, who had before

Gained fame, rode round to every Mirador;
Beneath each lady's stand a stop he made,
And, bowing, took the applauses which they paid.
Just in that point of time, the brave unknown
Approached the lists.

BOABDELIN
I marked him, when alone
(Observed by all, himself observing none)
He entered first, and with a graceful pride
His fiery Arab dextrously did guide,
Who, while his rider every stand surveyed,
Sprung loose, and flew into an escapade;
Not moving forward, yet, with every bound,
Pressing, and seeming still to quit his ground.
What after passed
Was far from the Ventanna where I sate,
But you were near, and can the truth relate. [To **ABDELMELECH**.

ABDELMELECH
Thus while he stood, the bull, who saw his foe,
His easier conquests proudly did forego;
And, making at him with a furious bound,
From his bent forehead aimed a double wound.
A rising murmur ran through all the field,
And every lady's blood with fear was chilled:
Some shrieked, while others, with more helpful care,
Cried out aloud,—Beware, brave youth, beware!
At this he turned, and, as the bull drew near,
Shunned, and received him on his pointed spear:
The lance broke short, the beast then bellowed loud,
And his strong neck to a new onset bowed.
The undaunted youth
Then drew; and, from his saddle bending low,
Just where the neck did to the shoulders grow,
With his full force discharged a deadly blow.
Not heads of poppies (when they reap the grain)
Fall with more ease before the labouring swain,
Than fell this head:
It fell so quick, it did even death prevent,
And made imperfect bellowings as it went.
Then all the trumpets victory did sound,
And yet their clangors in our shouts were drown'd.

[A confused noise within.

BOABDELIN
The alarm-bell rings from our Alhambra walls,

And from the streets sound drums and ataballes.

[Within, a bell, drums, and trumpets.

[Enter a **MESSENGER**.

How now? from whence proceed these new alarms?

MESSENGER
The two fierce factions are again in arms;
And, changing into blood the day's delight,
The Zegrys with the Abencerrages fight;
On each side their allies and friends appear;
The Macas here, the Alabezes there:
The Gazuls with the Bencerrages join,
And, with the Zegrys, all great Gomel's line.

BOABDELIN
Draw up behind the Vivarambla place;
Double my guards,—these factions I will face;
And try if all the fury they can bring,
Be proof against the presence of their king.

[Exit **BOABDELIN**.

[The Factions appear: At the head of the Abencerrages, **OZMYN**; at the head of the Zegrys, **ULEMA**, **HAMET**, **GOMEL**, and **SELIN**: **ABENAMAR** and **ABDELMELECH**, joined with the Abencerrages.

ZULEMA
The faint Abencerrages quit their ground:
Press them; put home your thrusts to every wound.

ABDELMELECH
Zegry, on manly force our line relies;
Thine poorly takes the advantage of surprise:
Unarmed and much out-numbered we retreat;
You gain no fame, when basely you defeat.
If thou art brave, seek nobler victory;
Save Moorish blood; and, while our bands stand by,
Let two and two an equal combat try.

HAMET
'Tis not for fear the combat we refuse,
But we our gained advantage will not lose.

ZULEMA
In combating, but two of you will fall;
And we resolve we will dispatch you all.

OZMYN

We'll double yet the exchange before we die,
And each of ours two lives of yours shall buy.

[**ALMANZOR** enters betwixt them, as they stand ready to engage.

ALMANZOR

I cannot stay to ask which cause is best;
But this is so to me, because opprest.

[Goes to the **ABENAMAR**.

[To them B**OABDELIN** and his **GUARDS**, going betwixt them.

BOABDELIN

On your allegiance, I command you stay;
Who passes here, through me must make his way;
My life's the Isthmus; through this narrow line
You first must cut, before those seas can join.
What fury, Zegrys, has possessed your minds?
What rage the brave Abencerrages blinds?
If of your courage you new proofs would show,
Without much travel you may find a foe.
Those foes are neither so remote nor few,
That you should need each other to pursue.
Lean times and foreign wars should minds unite;
When poor, men mutter, but they seldom fight.
O holy Alha! that I live to see
Thy Granadines assist their enemy!
You fight the christians' battles; every life
You lavish thus, in this intestine strife,
Does from our weak foundations take one prop,
Which helped to hold our sinking country up.

OZMYN

'Tis fit our private enmity should cease;
Though injured first, yet I will first seek peace.

ZULEMA

No, murderer, no; I never will be won
To peace with him, whose hand has slain my son.

OZMYN

Our prophet's curse
On me, and all the Abencerrages light,
If, unprovoked, I with your son did fight.

ABDELMELECH

A band of Zegrys ran within the place,
Matched with a troop of thirty of our race.
Your son and Ozmyn the first squadrons led,
Which, ten by ten, like Parthians, charged and fled.
The ground was strowed with canes where we did meet,
Which crackled underneath our coursers' feet:
When Tarifa (I saw him ride a part)
Changed his blunt cane for a steel-pointed dart,
And, meeting Ozmyn next,—
Who wanted time for treason to provide,—
He basely threw it at him, undefied.

OZMYN [Shewing his arms.]

Witness this blood—which when by treason sought,
That followed, sir, which to myself I ought.

ZULEMA

His hate to thee was grounded on a grudge,
Which all our generous Zegrys just did judge:
Thy villain-blood thou openly didst place
Above the purple of our kingly race.

BOABDELIN

From equal stems their blood both houses draw,
They from Morocco, you from Cordova.

HAMET

Their mongrel race is mixed with Christian breed;
Hence 'tis that they those dogs in prisons feed.

ABDELMELECH

Our holy prophet wills, that charity
Should even to birds and beasts extended be:
None knows what fate is for himself designed;
The thought of human chance should make us kind.

GOMEL

We waste that time we to revenge should give:
Fall on: let no Abencerrago live.

[Advancing before the rest of his party. **ALMANZOR** advancing on the other side, and describing a line with his sword.

ALMANZOR

Upon thy life pass not this middle space;
Sure death stands guarding the forbidden place.

GOMEL
To dare that death, I will approach yet nigher;
Thus,—wert thou compassed in with circling fire.

[They fight.

BOABDELIN
Disarm them both; if they resist you, kill.

[**ALMANZOR**, in the midst of the guards, kills **GOMEL**, and then is disarmed.

ALMANZOR
Now you have but the leavings of my will.

BOABDELIN
Kill him! this insolent unknown shall fall,
And be the victim to atone you all.

OZMYN
If he must die, not one of us will live:
That life he gave for us, for him we give.

BOABDELIN
It was a traitor's voice that spoke those words;
So are you all, who do not sheath your swords.

ZULEMA
Outrage unpunished, when a prince is by,
Forfeits to scorn the rights of majesty:
No subject his protection can expect,
Who what he owes himself does first neglect.

ABENAMAR
This stranger, sir, is he,
Who lately in the Vivarambla place
Did, with so loud applause, your triumphs grace.

BOABDELIN
The word which I have given, I'll not revoke;
If he be brave, he's ready for the stroke.

ALMANZOR
No man has more contempt than I of breath,
But whence hast thou the right to give me death?
Obeyed as sovereign by thy subjects be,
But know, that I alone am king of me.
I am as free as nature first made man,
Ere the base laws of servitude began,

When wild in woods the noble savage ran.

BOABDELIN
Since, then, no power above your own you know,
Mankind should use you like a common foe;
You should be hunted like a beast of prey:
By your own law I take your life away.

ALMANZOR
My laws are made but only for my sake;
No king against himself a law can make.
If thou pretend'st to be a prince like me,
Blame not an act, which should thy pattern be.
I saw the oppressed, and thought it did belong
To a king's office to redress the wrong:
I brought that succour, which thou ought'st to bring,
And so, in nature, am thy subjects' king.

BOABDELIN
I do not want your counsel to direct
Or aid to help me punish or protect.

ALMANZOR
Thou want'st them both, or better thou would'st know,
Than to let factions in thy kingdom grow.
Divided interests, while thou think'st to sway,
Draw, like two brooks, thy middle stream away:
For though they band and jar, yet both combine
To make their greatness by the fall of thine.
Thus, like a buckler, thou art held in sight,
While they behind thee with each other fight.

BOABDELIN [To his **GUARDS**.]
Away, and execute him instantly!

ALMANZOR
Stand off; I have not leisure yet to die.

[To them, enter **ABDALLA** hastily.

ABDALLA
Hold, sir! for heaven's sake hold!
Defer this noble stranger's punishment,
Or your rash orders you will soon repent.

BOABDELIN
Brother, you know not yet his insolence.

ABDALLA

Upon yourself you punish his offence:
If we treat gallant strangers in this sort,
Mankind will shun the inhospitable court;
And who, henceforth, to our defence will come,
If death must be the brave Almanzor's doom?
From Africa I drew him to your aid,
And for his succour have his life betrayed.

BOABDELIN

Is this the Almanzor whom at Fez you knew,
When first their swords the Xeriff brothers drew?

ABDALLA

This, sir, is he, who for the elder fought,
And to the juster cause the conquest brought;
Till the proud Santo, seated on the throne,
Disdained the service he had done to own:
Then to the vanquished part his fate he led;
The vanquished triumphed, and the victor fled.
Vast is his courage, boundless is his mind,
Rough as a storm, and humorous as wind:
Honour's the only idol of his eyes;
The charms of beauty like a pest he flies;
And, raised by valour from a birth unknown,
Acknowledges no power above his own.

[**BOABDELIN** coming to **ALMANZOR**.

BOABDELIN

Impute your danger to our ignorance;
The bravest men are subject most to chance:
Granada much does to your kindness owe;
But towns, expecting sieges, cannot show
More honour, than to invite you to a foe.

ALMANZOR

I do not doubt but I have been to blame:
But, to pursue the end for which I came,
Unite your subjects first; then let us go,
And pour their common rage upon the foe.

BOABDELIN [to the Factions.]
Lay down your arms, and let me beg you cease
Your enmities.

ZULEMA
We will not hear of peace,

Till we by force have first revenged our slain.

ABDELMELECH
The action we have done we will maintain.

SELIN
Then let the king depart, and we will try
Our cause by arms.

ZULEMA
For us and victory.

BOABDELIN
A king entreats you.

ALMANZOR
What subjects will precarious kings regard?
A beggar speaks too softly to be heard:
Lay down your arms! 'tis I command you now.
Do it—or, by our prophet's soul I vow,
My hands shall right your king on him I seize.
Now let me see whose look but disobeys.

OMNES
Long live king Mahomet Boabdelin!

ALMANZOR
No more; but hushed as midnight silence go:
He will not have your acclamations now.
Hence, you unthinking crowd!—

[The Common **PEOPLE** go off on both parties.

Empire, thou poor and despicable thing,
When such as these make or unmake a king!

ABDALLA
How much of virtue lies in one great soul,

[Embracing him.

Whose single force can multitudes controul!

[A trumpet within.

[Enter a **MESSENGER**.

MESSENGER

The Duke of Arcos, sir,
Does with a trumpet from the foe appear.

BOABDELIN
Attend him; he shall have his audience here.

[Enter the **Duke of ARCOS.**

Duke of ARCOS
The monarchs of Castile and Arragon
Have sent me to you, to demand this town.
To which their just and rightful claim is known.

BOABDELIN
Tell Ferdinand, my right to it appears
By long possession of eight hundred years:
When first my ancestors from Afric sailed,
In Rodrique's death your Gothic title failed.

Duke of ARCOS
The successors of Rodrique still remain,
And ever since have held some part of Spain:
Even in the midst of your victorious powers,
The Asturias, and all Portugal, were ours.
You have no right, except you force allow;
And if yours then was just, so ours is now.

BOABDELIN
'Tis true from force the noblest title springs;
I therefore hold from that, which first made kings.

Duke of ARCOS
Since then by force you prove your title true,
Ours must be just, because we claim from you.
When with your father you did jointly reign,
Invading with your Moors the south of Spain,
I, who that day the Christians did command,
Then took, and brought you bound to Ferdinand.

BOABDELIN
I'll hear no more; defer what you would say;
In private we'll discourse some other day.

Duke of ARCOS
Sir, you shall hear, however you are loth,
That, like a perjured prince, you broke your oath:
To gain your freedom you a contract signed,
By which your crown you to my king resigned,

From thenceforth as his vassal holding it,
And paying tribute such as he thought fit;
Contracting, when your father came to die,
To lay aside all marks of royalty,
And at Purchena privately to live,
Which, in exchange, king Ferdinand did give.

BOABDELIN
The force used on me made that contract void.

Duke of ARCOS
Why have you then its benefits enjoyed?
By it you had not only freedom then,
But, since, had aid of money and of men;
And, when Granada for your uncle held,
You were by us restored, and he expelled.
Since that, in peace we let you reap your grain,
Recalled our troops, that used to beat your plain;
And more—

ALMANZOR
Yes, yes, you did, with wonderous care,
Against his rebels prosecute the war,
While he secure in your protection slept;
For him you took, but for yourself you kept.
Thus, as some fawning usurer does feed,
With present sums, the unwary spendthrift's need,
You sold your kindness at a boundless rate,
And then o'erpaid the debt from his estate;
Which, mouldering piecemeal, in your hands did fall,
Till now at last you come to swoop it all.

Duke of ARCOS
The wrong you do my king, I cannot bear;
Whose kindness you would odiously compare.—
The estate was his; which yet, since you deny,
He's now content, in his own wrong, to buy.

ALMANZOR
And he shall buy it dear! What his he calls,
We will not give one stone from out these walls.

BOABDELIN
Take this for answer, then,—
Whate'er your arms have conquered of my land,
I will, for peace, resign to Ferdinand.—
To harder terms my mind I cannot bring;
But, as I still have lived, will die a king.

Duke of ARCOS
Since thus you have resolved, henceforth prepare
For all the last extremities of war:
My king his hope from heaven's assistance draws.

ALMANZOR
The Moors have heaven, and me, to assist their cause.

[Exit **Duke of ARCOS**.

[Enter **ESPERANZA**.

ESPERANZA
Fair Almahide,
(Who did with weeping eyes these discords see,
And fears the omen may unlucky be,)
Prepares a zambra to be danced this night.
In hope soft pleasures may your minds unite.

BOABDELIN
My mistress gently chides the fault I made:
But tedious business has my love delayed,—
Business which dares the joys of kings invade.

ALMANZOR
First let us sally out, and meet the foe.

ABDALLA
Led on by you, we on to triumph go.

BOABDELIN
Then with the day let war and tumult cease;
The night be sacred to our love and peace:
'Tis just some joys on weary kings should wait;
'Tis all we gain by being slaves to state.

[Exeunt.

ACT II

SCENE I

Enter **ABDALLA, ABDELMELECH, OZMYN, ZULEMA**, and **HAMET**, as returning from the sally.

ABDALLA

This happy day does to Granada bring
A lasting peace, and triumphs to the king!—
The two fierce factions will no longer jar,
Since they have now been brothers in the war.
Those who, apart, in emulation fought,
The common danger to one body brought;
And, to his cost, the proud Castilian finds
Our Moorish courage in united minds.

ABDELMELECH
Since to each others aid our lives we owe,
Lose we the name of faction, and of foe;
Which I to Zulema can bear no more,
Since Lyndaraxa's beauty I adore.

ZULEMA
I am obliged to Lyndaraxa's charms,
Which gain the conquest I should lose by arms;
And wish my sister may continue fair,
That I may keep a good,
Of whose possession I should else despair.

OZMYN
While we indulge our common happiness,
He is forgot, by whom we all possess;
The brave Almanzor, to whose arms we owe
All that we did, and all that we shall do;
Who, like a tempest, that out-rides the wind,
Made a just battle ere the bodies joined.

ABDELMELECH
His victories we scarce could keep in view,
Or polish them so fast as he rough-drew.

ABDALLA
Fate, after him, below with pain did move,
And victory could scarce keep pace above:
Death did at length so many slain forget,
And lost the tale, and took them by the great.

[Enter **ALMANZOR**, with the **Duke of ARCOS**, prisoner.

HAMET
See, here he comes,
And leads in triumph him, who did command
The vanquished army of king Ferdinand.

ALMANZOR [To the **Duke of ARCOS**.]

Thus far your master's arms a fortune find
Below the swelled ambition of his mind;
And Alha shuts a misbeliever's reign
From out the best and goodliest part of Spain.
Let Ferdinand Calabrian conquests make,
And from the French contested Milan take;
Let him new worlds discover to the old,
And break up shining mountains, big with gold;
Yet he shall find this small domestic foe,
Still sharp and pointed, to his bosom grow.

Duke of ARCOS
Of small advantages too much you boast;
You beat the out-guards of my master's host:
This little loss, in our vast body, shows
So small, that half have never heard the news.
Fame's out of breath, ere she can fly so far,
To tell them all, that you have e'er made war.

ALMANZOR
It pleases me your army is so great;
For now I know there's more to conquer yet.
By heaven! I'll see what troops you have behind:
I'll face this storm, that thickens in the wind;
And, with bent forehead, full against it go,
'Till I have found the last and utmost foe.

Duke of ARCOS
Believe, you shall not long attend in vain:
To-morrow's dawn shall cover all the plain;
Bright arms shall flash upon you from afar,
A wood of lances, and a moving war.
But I, unhappy, in my bonds, must yet
Be only pleased to hear of your defeat,
And with a slave's inglorious ease remain,
'Till conquering Ferdinand has broke my chain.

ALMANZOR
Vain man, thy hopes of Ferdinand are weak!
I hold thy chain too fast for him to break.
But, since thou threaten'st us, I'll set thee free,
That I again may fight, and conquer thee.

Duke of ARCOS
Old as I am, I take thee at thy word,
And will to-morrow thank thee with my sword.

ALMANZOR

I'll go, and instantly acquaint the king,
And sudden orders for thy freedom bring.
Thou canst not be so pleased at liberty,
As I shall be to find thou darest be free.

[Exeunt **ALMANZOR, ARCOS,** and the rest, excepting only **ABDALLA** and **ZULEMA.**

ABDALLA
Of all those Christians who infest this town,
This duke of Arcos is of most renown.

ZULEMA
Oft have I heard, that, in your father's reign,
His bold adventurers beat the neighbouring plain;
Then under Ponce Leon's name he fought,
And from our triumphs many prizes brought;
Till in disgrace from Spain at length he went,
And since continued long in banishment.

ABDALLA
But, see, your beauteous sister does appear.

[Enter **LYNDARAXA.**

ZULEMA
By my desire she came to find me here.

[**ZULEMA** and **LYNDARAXA** whisper; then **ZULEMA** goes out, and **LYNDARAXA** is going after.

ABDALLA
Why, fairest Lyndaraxa, do you fly

[Staying her.

A prince, who at your feet is proud to die?

LYNDARAXA
Sir, I should blush to own so rude a thing,

[Staying.

As 'tis to shun the brother of my king.

ABDALLA
In my hard fortune, I some ease should find,
Did your disdain extend to all mankind.
But give me leave to grieve, and to complain,
That you give others what I beg in vain.

LYNDARAXA

Take my esteem, if you on that can live;
For, frankly, sir, 'tis all I have to give:
If from my heart you ask or hope for more,
I grieve the place is taken up before.

ABDALLA

My rival merits you.—
To Abdelmelech I will justice do;
For he wants worth, who dares not praise a foe.

LYNDARAXA

That for his virtue, sir, you make defence,
Shows in your own a noble confidence.
But him defending, and excusing me,
I know not what can your advantage be.

ABDALLA

I fain would ask, ere I proceed in this,
If, as by choice, you are by promise his?

LYNDARAXA

The engagement only in my love does lie,
But that's a knot which you can ne'er untie.

ABDALLA

When cities are besieged, and treat to yield,
If there appear relievers from the field,
The flag of parley may be taken down,
Till the success of those without is known;

LYNDARAXA

Though Abdelmelech has not yet possest,
Yet I have sealed the treaty in my breast.

ABDALLA

Your treaty has not tied you to a day;
Some chance might break it, would you but delay.
If I can judge the secrets of your heart,
Ambition in it has the greatest part;
And wisdom, then, will shew some difference,
Betwixt a private person, and a prince.

LYNDARAXA

Princes are subjects still.—
Subject and subject can small difference bring:
The difference is 'twixt subjects and a king.

And since, sir, you are none, your hopes remove;
For less than empire I'll not change my love.

ABDALLA
Had I a crown, all I should prize in it,
Should be the power to lay it at your feet.

LYNDARAXA
Had you that crown, which you but wish, not hope,
Then I, perhaps, might stoop, and take it up.
But till your wishes and your hopes agree,
You shall be still a private man with me.

ABDALLA
If I am king, and if my brother die,—

LYNDARAXA
Two if's scarce make one possibility.

ABDALLA
The rule of happiness by reason scan;
You may be happy with a private man.

LYNDARAXA
That happiness I may enjoy, 'tis true;
But then that private man must not be you.
Where'er I love, I'm happy in my choice;
If I make you so, you shall pay my price.

ABDALLA
Why would you be so great?

LYNDARAXA
Because I've seen,
This day, what 'tis to hope to be a queen.—
Heaven, how you all watched each motion of her eye!
None could be seen while Almahide was by,
Because she is to be—her majesty!—
Why would I be a queen? Because my face
Would wear the title with a better grace.
If I became it not, yet it would be
Part of your duty, then, to flatter me.
These are but half the charms of being great;
I would be somewhat, that I know not yet:—
Yes! I avow the ambition of my soul,
To be that one to live without controul!
And that's another happiness to me,
To be so happy as but one can be.

ABDALLA

Madam,—because I would all doubts remove,—
Would you, were I a king, accept my love?

LYNDARAXA

I would accept it; and, to shew 'tis true,
From any other man as soon as you.

ABDALLA

Your sharp replies make me not love you less;
But make me seek new paths to happiness.—
What I design, by time will best be seen:
You may be mine, and yet may be a queen.
When you are so, your word your love assures.

LYNDARAXA

Perhaps not love you,—but I will be yours.—

[He offers to take her hand, and kiss it.

Stay, sir, that grace I cannot yet allow;
Before you set the crown upon my brow.—
That favour which you seek,
Or Abdelmelech, or a king, must have;
When you are so, then you may be my slave.

[Exit; but looks smiling back on him.

ABDALLA

Howe'er imperious in her words she were,
Her parting looks had nothing of severe;
A glancing smile allured me to command,
And her soft fingers gently pressed my hand:
I felt the pleasure glide through every part;
Her hand went through me to my very heart.
For such another pleasure, did he live,
I could my father of a crown deprive.—
What did I say?—
Father!—That impious thought has shocked my mind:
How bold our passions are, and yet how blind!—
She's gone; and now,
Methinks, there is less glory in a crown:
My boiling passions settle, and go down.
Like amber chafed, when she is near, she acts;
When farther oft, inclines, but not attracts.

[Enter **ZULEMA**.

Assist me, Zulema, if thou wouldst be
That friend thou seem'st, assist me against me.
Betwixt my love and virtue I am tossed;
This must be forfeited, or that be lost.
I could do much to merit thy applause,—
Help me to fortify the better cause;
My honour is not wholly put to flight,
But would, if seconded, renew the fight.

ZULEMA

I met my sister, but I do not see
What difficulty in your choice can be:
She told me all; and 'tis so plain a case,
You need not ask what counsel to embrace.

ABDALLA

I stand reproved, that I did doubt at all;
My waiting virtue staid but for thy call:
'Tis plain that she, who, for a kingdom, now
Would sacrifice her love, and break her vow,
Not out of love, but interest, acts alone,
And would, even in my arms, lie thinking of a throne.

ZULEMA

Add to the rest, this one reflection more:
When she is married, and you still adore,
Think then,—and think what comfort it will bring,—
She had been mine,
Had I but only dared to be a king!

ABDALLA

I hope you only would my honour try;
I'm loth to think you virtue's enemy.

ZULEMA

If, when a crown and mistress are in place,
Virtue intrudes, with her lean holy face,
Virtue's then mine, and not I virtue's foe.
Why does she come where she has nought to do?
Let her with anchorites, not with lovers, lie;
Statesmen and they keep better company.

ABDALLA

Reason was given to curb our head-strong will.

ZULEMA

Reason but shews a weak physician's skill;

Gives nothing, while the raging fit does last,
But stays to cure it, when the worst is past.
Reason's a staff for age, when nature's gone;
But youth is strong enough to walk alone,

ABDALLA

In cursed ambition I no rest should find,
But must for ever lose my peace of mind.

ZULEMA

Methinks that peace of mind were bravely lost;
A crown, whate'er we give, is worth the cost.

ABDALLA

Justice distributes to each man his right;
But what she gives ñot, should I take by might?

ZULEMA

If justice will take all, and nothing give,
Justice, methinks, is not distributive.

ABDALLA

Had fate so pleased, I had been eldest born,
And then, without a crime, the crown had worn!—

ZULEMA

Would you so please, fate yet a way would find;
Man makes his fate according to his mind.
The weak low spirit, fortune makes her slave;
But she's a drudge, when hectored by the brave:
If fate weaves common thread, he'll change the doom,
And with new purple spread a nobler loom.

ABDALLA

No more!—I will usurp the royal seat;
Thou, who hast made me wicked, make me great.

ZULEMA

Your way is plain: the death of Tarifa
Does on the king our Zegrys' hatred draw;
Though with our enemies in show we close,
'Tis but while we to purpose can be foes.
Selin, who heads us, would revenge his son;
But favour hinders justice to be done.
Proud Ozmyn with the king his power maintains,
And, in him, each Abencerrago reigns.

ABDALLA

What face of any title can I bring?

ZULEMA

The right an eldest son has to be king.
Your father was at first a private man,
And got your brother ere his reign began;
When, by his valour, he the crown had won,
Then you were born a monarch's eldest son.

ABDALLA

To sharp-eyed reason this would seem untrue;
But reason I through love's false optics view.

ZULEMA

Love's mighty power has led me captive too;
I am in it unfortunate as you.

ABDALLA

Our loves and fortunes shall together go;
Thou shalt be happy, when I first am so.

ZULEMA

The Zegrys at old Selin's house are met,
Where, in close council, for revenge they sit:
There we our common interest will unite;
You their revenge shall own, and they your right.
One thing I had forgot, which may import:
I met Almanzor coming back from court,
But with a discomposed and speedy pace,
A fiery colour kindling all his face:
The king his prisoner's freedom has denied,
And that refusal has provoked his pride.

ABDALLA

'Would he were ours!—
I'll try to gild the injustice of his cause,
And court his valour with a vast applause.

ZULEMA

The bold are but the instruments o'the wise;
They undertake the dangers we advise:
And, while our fabric with their pains we raise,
We take the profit, and pay them with praise.

[Exeunt.

Enter **ALMANZOR** and **ABDALLA**.

ALMANZOR
That he should dare to do me this disgrace!—
Is fool, or coward, writ upon my face?
Refuse my prisoner!—I such means will use,
He shall not have a prisoner to refuse.

ABDALLA
He said, you were not by your promise tied;
That he absolved your word, when he denied.

ALMANZOR
He break my promise, and absolve my vow!
'Tis more than Mahomet himself can do!—
The word, which I have given, shall stand like fate;
Not like the king's, that weather-cock of state.
He stands so high, with so unfixed a mind,
Two factions turn him with each blast of wind:
But now, he shall not veer! my word is past;
I'll take his heart by the roots, and hold it fast.

ABDALLA
You have your vengeance in your hand this hour;
Make me the humble creature of your power:
The Granadines will gladly me obey;
(Tired with so base and impotent a sway)
And, when I shew my title, you shall see,
I have a better right to reign than he.

ALMANZOR
It is sufficient that you make the claim;
You wrong our friendship when your right you name.
When for myself I fight, I weigh the cause;
But friendship will admit of no such laws:
That weighs by the lump; and, when the cause is light,
Puts kindness in to set the balance right.
True, I would wish my friend the juster side;
But, in the unjust, my kindness more is tried:
And all the opposition I can bring,
Is, that I fear to make you such a king.

ABDALLA
The majesty of kings we should not blame,

When royal minds adorn the royal name;
The vulgar, greatness too much idolize,
But haughty subjects it too much despise.

ALMANZOR
I only speak of him,
Whom pomp and greatness sit so loose about,
That he wants majesty to fill them out.

ABDALLA
Haste, then, and lose no time!—
The business must be enterprised this night:
We must surprise the court in its delight.

ALMANZOR
For you to will, for me 'tis to obey:
But I would give a crown in open day;
And, when the Spaniards their assault begin,
At once beat those without, and these within.

[Exit **ALMANZOR**.

[Enter **ABDELMELECH**.

ABDELMELECH
Abdalla, hold!—There's somewhat I intend
To speak, not as your rival, but your friend.

ABDALLA
If as a friend, I am obliged to hear;
And what a rival says I cannot fear.

ABDELMELECH
Think, brave Abdalla, what it is you do:
Your quiet, honour, and our friendship too,
All for a fickle beauty you forego.
Think, and turn back, before it be too late.
Behold in me the example of your fate:
I am your sea-mark; and, though wrecked and lost,
My ruins stand to warn you from the coast.

ABDALLA
Your counsels, noble Abdelmelech, move
My reason to accept them, not my love.
Ah, why did heaven leave man so weak defence,
To trust frail reason with the rule of sense!
'Tis over-poised and kicked up in the air,
While sense weighs down the scale, and keeps it there;

Or, like a captive king, 'tis borne away,
And forced to countenance its own rebels' sway.

ABDELMELECH

No, no; our reason was not vainly lent;
Nor is a slave, but by its own consent:
If reason on his subject's triumph wait,
An easy king deserves no better fate.

ABDALLA

You speak too late; my empire's lost too far:
I cannot fight.

ABDELMELECH

Then make a flying war;
Dislodge betimes, before you are beset.

ABDALLA

Her tears, her smiles, her every look's a net.
Her voice is like a Syren's of the land;
And bloody hearts lie panting in her hand.

ABDELMELECH

This do you know, and tempt the danger still?

ABDALLA

Love, like a lethargy, has seized my will.
I'm not myself, since from her sight I went;
I lean my trunk that way, and there stand bent.
As one, who, in some frightful dream, would shun
His pressing foe, labours in vain to run;
And his own slowness, in his sleep, bemoans,
With thick short sighs, weak cries, and tender groans,
So I—

ABDELMELECH

Some friend, in charity, should shake,
And rouse, and call you loudly till you wake.
Too well I know her blandishments to gain,
Usurper-like, till settled in her reign;
Then proudly she insults, and gives you cares,
And jealousies, short hopes, and long despairs.
To this hard yoke you must hereafter bow,
Howe'er she shines all golden to you now.

ABDALLA

Like him, who on the ice
Slides swiftly on, and sees the water near,

Yet cannot stop himself in his career,
So am I carried. This enchanted place,
Like Circe's isle, is peopled with a race
Of dogs and swine; yet, though their fate I know,
I look with pleasure, and am turning too.

[**LYNDARAXA** passes over the Stage.

ABDELMELECH
Fly, fly, before the allurements of her face,
Ere she return with some resistless grace,
And with new magic cover all the place.

ABDALLA
I cannot, will not,—nay, I would not fly:
I'll love, be blind, be cozened till I die;
And you, who bid me wiser counsel take,
I'll hate, and, if I can, I'll kill you for her sake.

ABDELMELECH
Even I, that counselled you, that choice approve:
I'll hate you blindly, and her blindly love.
Prudence, that stemmed the stream, is out of breath:
And to go down it is the easier death.

[**LYNDARAXA** re-enters, and smiles on **ABDALLA**.

[Exit **ABDALLA**.

ABDELMELECH
That smile on Prince Abdalla seems to say,
You are not in your killing mood to day:
Men brand, indeed, your sex with cruelty,
But you are too good to see poor lovers die.
This god-like pity in you I extol;
And more, because, like heaven's, 'tis general.

LYNDARAXA
My smile implies not that I grant his suit:
'Twas but a bare return of his salute.

ABDELMELECH
It said, you were engaged, and I in place;
But, to please both, you would divide the grace.

LYNDARAXA
You've cause to be contented with your part,
When he has but the look, and you the heart.

ABDELMELECH

In giving but that look, you give what's mine:
I'll not one corner of a glance resign.
All's mine; and I am covetous of my store:
I have not love enough, I'll tax you more.

LYNDARAXA

I gave not love; 'twas but civility:
He is a prince; that's due to his degree.

ABDELMELECH

That prince you smiled on is my rival still,
And should, if me you loved, be treated ill.

LYNDARAXA

I know not how to show so rude a spite.

ABDELMELECH

That is, you know not how to love aright;
Or, if you did, you would more difference see
Betwixt our souls, than 'twixt our quality.
Mark, if his birth makes any difference,
If to his words it adds one grain of sense.
That duty, which his birth can make his due,
I'll pay, but it shall not be paid by you:
For, if a prince courts her whom I adore,
He is my rival, and a prince no more.

LYNDARAXA

And when did I my power so far resign.
That you should regulate each look of mine?

ABDELMELECH

Then, when you gave your love, you gave that power.

LYNDARAXA

'Twas during pleasure, 'tis revoked this hour.
Now, call me false, and rail on womankind,—
'Tis all the remedy you're like to find.

ABDELMELECH

Yes, there's one more;
I'll hate you, and this visit is my last.

LYNDARAXA

Do't, if you can; you know I hold you fast:
Yet, for your quiet, would you could resign

Your love, as easily as I do mine.

ABDELMELECH
Furies and hell, how unconcerned she speaks!
With what indifference all her vows she breaks!
Curse on me, but she smiles!

LYNDARAXA
That smile's a part of love, and all's your due:
I take it from the prince, and give it you.

ABDELMELECH
Just heaven, must my poor heart your May-game prove,
To bandy, and make children's play in love?
[Half crying.
Ah! how have I this cruelty deserved?
I, who so truly and so long have served!
And left so easily! oh cruel maid!
So easily! it was too unkindly said.
That heart, which could so easily remove,
Was never fixed, nor rooted deep in love.

LYNDARAXA
You lodged it so uneasy in your breast,
I thought you had been weary of the guest.
First, I was treated like a stranger there;
But, when a household friend I did appear,
You thought, it seems, I could not live elsewhere.
Then, by degrees, your feigned respect withdrew;
You marked my actions, and my guardian grew.
But I am not concerned your acts to blame:
My heart to yours but upon liking came;
And, like a bird, whom prying boys molest,
Stays not to breed, where she had built her nest.

ABDELMELECH
I have done ill,
And dare not ask you to be less displeased;
Be but more angry, and my pain is eased.

LYNDARAXA
If I should be so kind a fool, to take
This little satisfaction which you make,
I know you would presume some other time
Upon my goodness, and repeat your crime.

ABDELMELECH
Oh never, never, upon no pretence;

My life's too short to expiate this offence.

LYNDARAXA
No, now I think on't, 'tis in vain to try;
'Tis in your nature, and past remedy.
You'll still disquiet my too loving heart:
Now we are friends 'tis best for both to part.

[He takes her hand.

ABDELMELECH
By this—Will you not give me leave to swear?

LYNDARAXA
You would be perjured if you should, I fear:
And, when I talk with Prince Abdalla next,
I with your fond suspicions shall be vext.

ABDELMELECH
I cannot say I'll conquer jealousy,
But, if you'll freely pardon me, I'll try.

LYNDARAXA
And, till you that submissive servant prove,
I never can conclude you truly love.

[To them, the **KING, ALMAHIDE, ABENAMAR, ESPERANZA, GUARDS, ATTENDANTS**.

BOABDELIN
Approach, my Almahide, my charming fair,
Blessing of peace, and recompence of war.
This night is yours; and may your life still be
The same in joy, though not solemnity.

THE ZAMBRA DANCE.

SONG.

I.
Beneath a myrtle shade,
Which love for none, but happy lovers made,
I slept; and straight my love before me brought
Phyllis, the object of my waking thought.
Undressed she came my flames to meet,
While love strewed flowers beneath her feet;
Flowers which, so pressed by her, became more sweet.

II.

From the bright vision's head
A careless veil of lawn was loosely spread:
From her white temples fell her shaded hair
Like cloudy sunshine, not too brown nor fair;
Her hands, her lips, did love inspire;
Her every grace my heart did fire:
But most her eyes, which languished with desire.

III.
Ah, charming fair, said I,
How long can you my bliss and yours deny?
By nature and by love, this lonely shade
Was for revenge of suffering lovers made.
Silence and shades with love agree;
Both shelter you and favour me:
You cannot blush, because I cannot see.

IV.
No, let me die, she said,
Rather than lose the spotless name of maid!—
Faintly, methought, she spoke; for all the while
She bid me not believe her, with a smile.
Then die, said I: She still denied;
And is it thus, thus, thus, she cried,
You use a harmless maid?—and so she died!

V.
I waked, and straight I knew,
I loved so well, it made my dream prove true:
Fancy, the kinder mistress of the two,
Fancy had done what Phyllis would not do!
Ah, cruel nymph, cease your disdain,
While, I can dream you scorn in vain,—
Asleep or waking you must ease my pain.

[After the dance, a tumultuous noise of drums and trumpets.

[To them **OZMYN**; his sword drawn.

OZMYN
Arm, quickly arm; yet all, I fear, too late;
The enemy's already at the gate.

BOABDELIN
The Christians are dislodged; what foe is near?

OZMYN
The Zegrys are in arms, and almost here:

The streets with torches shine, with shoutings ring,
And Prince Abdalla is proclaimed the king.
What man could do, I have already done,
But bold Almanzor fiercely leads them on.

ABENAMAR
The Alhambra yet is safe in my command; [To the **KING**.
Retreat you thither, while their shock we stand.

BOABDELIN
I cannot meanly for my life provide;
I'll either perish in't, or stem this tide.
To guard the palace, Ozmyn, be your care:
If they o'ercome, no sword will hurt the fair.

OZMYN
I'll either die; or I'll make good the place.

ABDELMELECH
And I with these will bold Almanzor face.

[Exeunt all but the **LADIES**. An alarum within.

ALMAHIDE
What dismal planet did my triumphs light!
Discord the day, and death does rule the night:
The noise my soul does through my senses wound.

LYNDARAXA
Methinks it is a noble, sprightly sound,
The trumpet's clangor, and the clash of arms!
This noise may chill your blood, but mine it warms.

[Shouting and clashing of swords within.

We have already passed the Rubicon;
The dice are mine; now, fortune, for a throne!

[A shout within, and clashing of swords afar off.

The sound goes farther off, and faintly dies;
Curse of this going back, these ebbing cries!
Ye winds, waft hither sounds more strong and quick;
Beat faster, drums, and mingle deaths more thick.
I'll to the turrets of the palace go,
And add new fire to those that fight below:
Thence, hero-like, with torches by my side,
(Far be the omen, though) my love will guide.

No; like his better fortune I'll appear,
With open arms, loose veil, and flowing hair,
Just flying forward from my rolling sphere:
My smiles shall make Abdalla more than man;
Let him look up, and perish if he can.

[Exit.

[An alarum nearer: Then Enter **ALMANZOR** and **SELIN**, at the head of the Zegrys; **OZMYN** Prisoner.

ALMANZOR
We have not fought enough; they fly too soon;
And I am grieved the noble sport is done.
This only man, of all whom chance did bring

[Pointing to **OZMYN**.

To meet my arms, was worth the conquering.
His brave resistance did my fortune grace;
So slow, so threatning forward he gave place.
His chains be easy, and his usage fair.

SELIN
I beg you would commit him to my care.

ALMANZOR
Next, the brave Spaniard free without delay;
And with a convoy send him safe away.

[Exit a **GUARD**.

[To them **HAMET** and **OTHERS**.

Hamet. The king by me salutes you; and, to show
That to your valour he his crown does owe,
Would from your mouth I should the word receive,
And that to these you would your orders give.

ALMANZOR
He much o'er-rates the little I have done.

[**ALMANZOR** goes to the door, and there seems to give out orders, by sending **PEOPLE** several ways.

SELIN [to **OZMYN**]
Now, to revenge the murder of my son,
To morrow for thy certain death prepare;
This night I only leave thee to despair.

OZMYN

Thy idle menaces I do not fear:
My business was to die or conquer here.
Sister, for you I grieve I could no more:
My present state betrays my want of power;
But, when true courage is of force bereft,
Patience, the only fortitude, is left.

[Exit with **SELIN**.

ALMAHIDE

Ah, Esperanza, what for me remains
But death, or, worse than death, inglorious chains!

ESPERANZA

Madam, you must not to despair give place;
Heaven never meant misfortune to that face.
Suppose there were no justice in your cause,
Beauty's a bribe that gives her judges laws.
That you are brought to this deplored estate,
Is but the ingenious flattery of your fate;
Fate fears her succour, like an alms, to give;
And would you, God-like, from yourself should live.

ALMAHIDE

Mark but how terribly his eyes appear!
And yet there's something roughly noble there,
Which, in unfashioned nature, looks divine,
And, like a gem, does in the quarry shine.

[**ALMANZOR** returns; she falls at his feet, being veiled.

ALMAHIDE

Turn, mighty conqueror, turn your face this way,
Do not refuse to hear the wretched pray!

ALMANZOR

What business can this woman have with me?

ALMAHIDE

That of the afflicted to the Deity.
So may your arms success in battle find;
So may the mistress of your vows be kind,
If you have any; or, if you have none,
So may your liberty be still your own!

ALMANZOR

Yes, I will turn my face, but not my mind:

You bane and soft destruction of mankind,
What would you have with me?

ALMAHIDE
I beg the grace

[Unveiling.

You would lay by those terrors of your face.
Till calmness to your eyes you first restore,
I am afraid, and I can beg no more.

ALMANZOR [Looking fixedly on her.]
Well; my fierce visage shall not murder you.
Speak quickly, woman; I have much to do.

ALMAHIDE
Where should I find the heart to speak one word?
Your voice, sir, is as killing as your sword.
As you have left the lightning of your eye,
So would you please to lay your thunder by.

ALMANZOR
I'm pleased and pained, since first her eyes I saw,
As I were stung with some tarantula.
Arms, and the dusty field, I less admire,
And soften strangely in some new desire;
Honour burns in me not so fiercely bright,
But pale as fires when mastered by the light:
Even while I speak and look, I change yet more,
And now am nothing that I was before.
I'm numbed, and fixed, and scarce my eye-balls move:
I fear it is the lethargy of love!
'Tis he; I feel him now in every part:
Like a new lord he vaunts about my heart;
Surveys, in state, each corner of my breast,
While poor fierce I, that was, am dispossessed.
I'm bound; but I will rouse my rage again;
And, though no hope of liberty remain,
I'll fright my keeper when I shake my chain.
You are—[Angrily.

ALMAHIDE
I know I am your captive, sir.

ALMANZOR
You are—You shall—And I can scarce forbear—

ALMAHIDE

Alas!

ALMANZOR

'Tis all in vain; it will not do: [Aside.
I cannot now a seeming anger show:
My tongue against my heart no aid affords;
For love still rises up, and choaks my words.

ALMAHIDE

In half this time a tempest would be still.

ALMANZOR

'Tis you have raised that tempest in my will.
I wonnot love you; give me back my heart;
But give it, as you had it, fierce and brave.
It was not made to be a woman's slave,
But, lion-like, has been in desarts bred,
And, used to range, will ne'er be tamely led.
Restore its freedom to my fettered will,
And then I shall have power to use you ill.

ALMAHIDE

My sad condition may your pity move;
But look not on me with the eyes of love:—
I must be brief, though I have much to say.

ALMANZOR

No, speak; for I can hear you now all day.
Her sueing sooths me with a secret pride: [Softly.
A suppliant beauty cannot be denied: [Aside.
Even while I frown, her charms the furrows seize;
And I'm corrupted with the power to please.

ALMAHIDE

Though in your worth no cause of fear I see,
I fear the insolence of victory;
As you are noble, sir, protect me then
From the rude outrage of insulting men.

ALMANZOR

Who dares touch her I love? I'm all o'er love:
Nay, I am love; love shot, and shot so fast,
He shot himself into my breast at last.

ALMAHIDE

You see before you her, who should be queen,
Since she is promised to Boabdelin.

ALMANZOR
Are you beloved by him? O wretched fate,
First that I love at all; then, loved too late!
Yet, I must love!

ALMAHIDE
Alas, it is in vain;
Fate for each other did not us ordain.
The chances of this day too clearly show
That heaven took care that it should not be so.

ALMANZOR
Would heaven had quite forgot me this one day!
But fate's yet hot—
I'll make it take a bent another way.

[He walks swiftly and discomposedly, studying.

I bring a claim which does his right remove;
You're his by promise, but you're mine by love.
'Tis all but ceremony which is past;
The knot's to tie which is to make you fast.
Fate gave not to Boabdelin that power;
He wooed you but as my ambassador.

ALMAHIDE
Our souls are tied by holy vows above.

ALMANZOR
He signed but his: but I will seal my love.
I love you better, with more zeal than he.

ALMAHIDE
This day
I gave my faith to him, he his to me.

ALMANZOR
Good heaven, thy book of fate before me lay,
But to tear out the journal of this day:
Or, if the order of the world below
Will not the gap of one whole day allow,
Give me that minute when she made her vow!
That minute, ev'n the happy from their bliss might give;
And those, who live in grief, a shorter time would live.
So small a link, if broke, the eternal chain
Would, like divided waters, join again.—
It wonnot be; the fugitive is gone,

Prest by the crowd of following minutes on:
That precious moment's out of nature fled,
And in the heap of common rubbish laid,
Of things that once have been, and are decayed.

ALMAHIDE
Your passion, like a fright, suspends my pain;
It meets, o'erpowers, and beats mine back again:
But as, when tides against the current flow,
The native stream runs its own course below,
So, though your griefs possess the upper part,
My own have deeper channels in my heart.

ALMANZOR
Forgive that fury which my soul does move;
'Tis the essay of an untaught first love:
Yet rude, unfashioned truth it does express;
'Tis love just peeping in a hasty dress.
Retire, fair creature, to your needful rest;
There's something noble labouring in my breast:
This raging fire, which through the mass does move,
Shall purge my dross, and shall refine my love.

[Exeunt **ALMAHIDE** and **ESPERANZA**.

She goes, and I like my own ghost appear;
It is not living when she is not here.

[To him **ABDALLA** as King, attended.

ABDALLA
My first acknowledgments to heaven are due;
My next, Almanzor, let me pay to you.

ALMANZOR
A poor surprise, and on a naked foe,
Whatever you confess, is all you owe;
And I no merit own, or understand
That fortune did you justice by my hand:
Yet, if you will that little service pay
With a great favour, I can shew the way.

ABDALLA
I have a favour to demand of you;
That is, to take the thing for which you sue.

ALMANZOR
Then, briefly, thus: when I the Albayzyn won,

I found the beauteous Almahide alone,
Whose sad condition did my pity move;
And that compassion did produce my love.

ABDALLA
This needs no suit; in justice, I declare.
She is your captive by the right of war.

ALMANZOR
She is no captive then; I set her free;
And, rather than I will her jailor be,
I'll nobly lose her in her liberty.

ABDALLA
Your generosity I much approve;
But your excess of that shows want of love.

ALMANZOR
No, 'tis the excess of love which mounts so high,
That, seen far off, it lessens to the eye.
Had I not loved her, and had set her free,
That, sir, had been my generosity;
But 'tis exalted passion, when I show
I dare be wretched, not to make her so:
And, while another passion fills her breast,
I'll be all wretched rather than half blest.

ABDALLA
May your heroic act so prosperous be,
That Almahide may sigh you set her free.

[Enter **ZULEMA**.

ZULEMA
Of five tall towers which fortify this town,
All but the Alhambra your dominion own:
Now, therefore, boldly I confess a flame,
Which is excused in Almahide's name.
If you the merit of this night regard,
In her possession I have my reward.

ALMANZOR
She your reward! why, she's a gift so great,
That I myself have not deserved her yet;
And therefore, though I won her with my sword,
I have, with awe, my sacrilege restored.

ZULEMA

What you deserve
I'll not dispute, because I do not know;
This only I will say, she shall not go.

ALMANZOR

Thou, single, art not worth my answering:
But take what friends, what armies thou canst bring;
What worlds; and, when you are united all,
Then will I thunder in your ears,—She shall.

ZULEMA

I'll not one tittle of my right resign.—
Sir, your implicit promise made her mine;
When I, in general terms, my love did show,
You swore our fortunes should together go.

ABDALLA

The merits of the cause I'll not decide,
But, like my love, I would my gift divide.
Your equal titles then no longer plead;
But one of you, for love of me, recede.

ALMANZOR

I have receded to the utmost line,
When, by my free consent, she is not mine:
Then let him equally recede with me,
And both of us will join to set her free.

ZULEMA

If you will free your part of her, you may;
But, sir, I love not your romantic way.
Dream on, enjoy her soul, and set that free;
I'm pleased her person should be left for me.

ALMANZOR

Thou shalt not wish her thine; thou shalt not dare
To be so impudent, as to despair.

ZULEMA

The Zegrys, sir, are all concerned to see
How much their merit you neglect in me.

HAMET

Your slighting Zulema, this very hour
Will take ten thousand subjects from your power.

ALMANZOR

What are ten thousand subjects such as they?

If I am scorned—I'll take myself away.

ABDALLA
Since both cannot possess what both pursue,
I grieve, my friend, the chance should fall on you;
But when you hear what reason I can urge—

ALMANZOR
None, none that your ingratitude can purge.
Reason's a trick, when it no grant affords;
It stamps the face of majesty on words.

ABDALLA
Your boldness to your services I give:
Now take it, as your full reward,—to live.

ALMANZOR
To live!
If from thy hands alone my death can be,
I am immortal, and a god to thee.
If I would kill thee now, thy fate's so low,
That I must stoop ere I can give the blow:
But mine is fixed so far above thy crown,
That all thy men,
Piled on thy back, can never pull it down:
But, at my ease, thy destiny I send,
By ceasing from this hour to be thy friend.
Like heaven, I need but only to stand still.
And, not concurring to thy life, I kill.
Thou canst no title to my duty bring;
I'm not thy subject, and my soul's thy king.
Farewell. When I am gone,
There's not a star of thine dare stay with thee:
I'll whistle thy tame fortune after me;
And whirl fate with me wheresoe'er I fly,
As winds drive storms before them in the sky.

[Exit.

ZULEMA
Let not this insolent unpunished go;
Give your commands; your justice is too slow.

[**ZULEMA, HAMET,** and **OTHERS** are going after him.

ABDALLA
Stay, and what part he pleases let him take:
I know my throne's too strong for him to shake.

But my fair mistress I too long forget;
The crown I promised is not offered yet.
Without her presence all my joys are vain,
Empire a curse, and life itself a pain.

[Exeunt.

ACT IV

SCENE I

Enter **BOABDELIN, ABENAMAR**, and **GUARDS.**

BOABDELIN
Advise, or aid, but do not pity me:
No monarch born can fall to that degree.
Pity descends from kings to all below;
But can, no more than fountains, upward flow.
Witness, just heaven, my greatest grief has been,
I could not make your Almahide a queen.

ABENAMAR
I have too long the effects of fortune known,
Either to trust her smiles, or fear her frown.
Since in their first attempt you were not slain,
Your safety bodes you yet a second reign.
The people like a headlong torrent go,
And ev'ry dam they break, or overflow;
But, unopposed, they either lose their force,
Or wind, in volumes, to their former course.

BOABDELIN
In walls we meanly must our hopes inclose,
To wait our friends, and weary out our foes:
While Almahide
To lawless rebels is exposed a prey,
And forced the lustful victor to obey.

ABENAMAR
One of my blood, in rules of virtue bred!
Think better of her, and believe she's dead.

[Enter **ALMANZOR.**

BOABDELIN
We are betrayed, the enemy is here;

We have no farther room to hope or fear.

ALMANZOR
It is indeed Almanzor whom you see,
But he no longer is your enemy.
You were ungrateful, but your foes were more;
What your injustice lost you, theirs restore.
Make profit of my vengeance while you may,
My two-edged sword can cut the other way.—
I am your fortune, but am swift like her,
And turn my hairy front if you defer:
That hour, when you deliberate, is too late;
I point you the white moment of your fate.

ABENAMAR
Believe him sent as prince Abdalla's spy;
He would betray us to the enemy.

ALMANZOR
Were I, like thee, in cheats of state grown old,
(Those public markets, where, for foreign gold,
The poorest prince is to the richest sold)
Then thou mightst think me fit for that low part;
But I am yet to learn the statesman's art.
My kindness and my hate unmasked I wear;
For friends to trust, and enemies to fear.
My heart's so plain,
That men on every passing through may look,
Like fishes gliding in a crystal brook;
When troubled most, it does the bottom shew,
'Tis weedless all above, and rockless all below.

ABENAMAR
Ere he be trusted, let him then be tried;
He may be false, who once has changed his side.

ALMANZOR
In that you more accuse yourselves than me;
None who are injured can inconstant be.
You were inconstant, you, who did the wrong;
To do me justice does to me belong.
Great souls by kindness only can be tied;
Injured again, again I'll leave your side.
Honour is what myself, and friends, I owe;
And none can lose it who forsake a foe.
Since, then, your foes now happen to be mine,
Though not in friendship, we'll in interest join:
So while my loved revenge is full and high,

I'll give you back your kingdom by the by.

BOABDELIN
That I so long delayed what you desire,

[Embracing him.

Was, not to doubt your worth, but to admire.

ALMANZOR
This counsellor an old man's caution shows,
Who fears that little, he has left, to lose:
Age sets a fortune; while youth boldly throws.
But let us first your drooping soldiers cheer;
Then seek out danger, ere it dare appear:
This hour I fix your crown upon your brow;
Next hour fate gives it, but I give it now.

[Exeunt.

SCENE II

Enter **LYNDARAXA**.

LYNDARAXA
O, could I read the dark decrees of fate,
That I might once know whom to love, or hate!
For I myself scarce my own thoughts can guess,
So much I find them varied by success.
As in some weather-glass, my love I hold;
Which falls or rises with the heat or cold.—
I will be constant yet, if fortune can;
I love the king,—let her but name the man.

[Enter **HALYMA**.

HALYMA
Madam, a gentleman, to me unknown,
Desires that he may speak with you alone.

LYNDARAXA
Some message from the king.—Let him appear.

[Enter **ABDELMELECH**; who throws off his disguise.—She starts.

ABDELMELECH

I see you are amazed that I am here:
But let at once your fear and wonder end.
In the usurper's guards I found a friend,
Who led me safe to you in this disguise.

LYNDARAXA

Your danger brings this trouble in my eyes.—
But what affair this 'venturous visit drew?

ABDELMELECH

The greatest in the world,—the seeing you.

LYNDARAXA

The courage of your love I so admire,
That, to preserve you, you shall straight retire.

[She leads him to the door.

Go, dear! each minute does new dangers bring;
You will be taken, I expect the king.

ABDELMELECH

The king!—the poor usurper of an hour:
His empire's but a dream of kingly power.—
I warn you, as a lover and a friend,
To leave him, ere his short dominion end:
The soldier I suborned will wait at night,
And shall alone be conscious of your flight.

LYNDARAXA

I thank you, that you so much care bestow;
But, if his reign be short, I need not go.
For why should I expose my life, and yours,
For what, you say, a little time assures?

ABDELMELECH

My danger in the attempt is very small;
And, if he loves you, yours is none at all.
But, though his ruin be as sure as fate,
Your proof of love to me would come too late.
This trial I in kindness would allow;
'Tis easy; if you love me, show it now.

LYNDARAXA

It is because I love you, I refuse;
For all the world my conduct would accuse,
If I should go with him I love away;
And, therefore, in strict virtue, I will stay.

ABDELMELECH

You would in vain dissemble love to me;
Through that thin veil your artifice I see.
You would expect the event, and then declare;
But do not, do not drive me to despair:
For, if you now refuse with me to fly,
Rather than love you after this, I'll die;
And, therefore, weigh it well before you speak;
My king is safe, his force within not weak.

LYNDARAXA

The counsel, you have given me, may be wise;
But, since the affair is great, I will advise.

ABDELMELECH

Then that delay I for denial take.

[Is going.

LYNDARAXA

Stay; you too swift an exposition make.
If I should go, since Zulema will stay,
I should my brother to the king betray.

ABDELMELECH

There is no fear; but, if there were, I see
You value still your brother more than me.—
Farewell! some ease I in your falsehood find;
It lets a beam in, that will clear my mind:
My former weakness I with shame confess,
And, when I see you next, shall love you less.

[Is going again.

LYNDARAXA

Your faithless dealings you may blush to tell:

[Weeping.

This is a maid's reward, who loves too well.—

[He looks back.

Remember that I drew my latest breath,
In charging your unkindness with my death.

ABDELMELECH [coming back]

Have I not answered all you can invent,
Even the least shadow of an argument?

LYNDARAXA
You want not cunning what you please to prove,
But my poor heart knows only how to love;
And, finding this, you tyrannize the more:
'Tis plain, some other mistress you adore;
And now, with studied tricks of subtlety,
You come prepared to lay the fault on me.

[Wringing her hands.

But, oh, that I should love so false a man!

ABDELMELECH
Hear me, and then disprove it, if you can.

LYNDARAXA
I'll hear no more; your breach of faith is plain:
You would with wit your want of love maintain.
But, by my own experience, I can tell,
They, who love truly, cannot argue well.—
Go faithless man!
Leave me alone to mourn my misery;
I cannot cease to love you, but I'll die.

[Leans her head on his arm.

ABDELMELECH
What man but I so long unmoved could hear

[Weeping.

Such tender passion, and refuse a tear!—
But do not talk of dying any more,
Unless you mean that I should die before.

LYNDARAXA
I fear your feigned repentance comes too late;
I die, to see you still thus obstinate:
But yet, in death my truth of love to show,
Lead me; if I have strength enough, I'll go.

ABDELMELECH
By heaven, you shall not go! I will not be
O'ercome in love or generosity.
All I desire, to end the unlucky strife,

Is but a vow, that you will be my wife.

LYNDARAXA
To tie me to you by a vow is hard;
It shows, my love you as no tie regard.—
Name any thing but that, and I'll agree.

ABDELMELECH
Swear, then, you never will my rival's be.

LYNDARAXA
Nay, pr'ythee, this is harder than before.—
Name any thing, good dear, but that thing more.

ABDELMELECH
Now I too late perceive I am undone;
Living and seeing, to my death I run.
I know you false, yet in your snares I fall;
You grant me nothing, and I grant you all.

LYNDARAXA
I would grant all; but I must curb my will,
Because I love to keep you jealous still.
In your suspicion I your passion find;
But I will take a time to cure your mind.

HALYMA
O, madam, the new king is drawing near!

LYNDARAXA
Haste quickly hence, lest he should find you here!

ABDELMELECH
How much more wretched than I came, I go!
I more my weakness and your falsehood know;
And now must leave you with my greatest foe!

[Exit **ABDELMELECH**.

LYNDARAXA
Go!—How I love thee heaven can only tell:
And yet I love thee, for a subject, well.—
Yet whatsoever charms a crown can bring,
A subject's greater than a little king.
I will attend till time this throne secure;
And, when I climb, my footing shall be sure.—

[Music without.

Music! and, I believe, addressed to me.

SONG.

I.

Wherever I am, and whatever I do,
My Phyllis is still in my mind;
When angry, I mean not to Phyllis to go,
My feet, of themselves, the way find:
Unknown to myself I am just at her door,
And, when I would rail, I can bring out no more
Than, Phyllis too fair and unkind!

II.

When Phyllis I see, my heart bounds in my breast,
And the love I would stifle is shown;
But asleep, or awake, I am never at rest,
When from my eyes Phyllis is gone.
Sometimes a sad dream does delude my sad mind;
But, alas! when I wake, and no Phyllis I find,
How I sigh to myself all alone!

III.

Should a king be my rival in her I adore,
He should offer his treasure in vain:
O, let me alone to be happy and poor,
And give me my Phyllis again!
Let Phyllis be mine, and but ever be kind,
I could to a desart with her be confined,
And envy no monarch his reign.

IV.

Alas! I discover too much of my love,
And she too well knows her own power!
She makes me each day a new martyrdom prove,
And makes me grow jealous each hour:
But let her each minute torment my poor mind,
I had rather love Phyllis, both false and unkind.
Than ever be freed from her power.

[Enter **ABDALLA**, with **GUARDS**.

ABDALLA

Now, madam, at your feet a king you see;
Or, rather, if you please, a sceptered slave:
'Tis just you should possess the power you gave.
Had love not made me yours, I yet had been

But the first subject to Boabdelin.
Thus heaven declares the crown I bring your due;
And had forgot my title, but for you.

LYNDARAXA
Heaven to your merits will, I hope, be kind;
But, sir, it has not yet declared its mind.
'Tis true, it holds the crown above your head;
But does not fix it 'till your brother's dead.

ABDALLA
All, but the Alhambra, is within my power;
And that my forces go to take this hour.

LYNDARAXA
When, with its keys, your brother's head you bring,
I shall believe you are indeed a king.

ABDALLA
But since the events of all things doubtful are,
And, of events, most doubtful those of war;
I beg to know before, if fortune frown,
Must I then lose your favour with my crown?

LYNDARAXA
You'll soon return a conqueror again;
And, therefore, sir, your question is in vain.

ABDALLA
I think to certain victory I move;
But you may more assure it, by your love.
That grant will make my arms invincible.

LYNDARAXA
My prayers and wishes your success foretell.—
Go then, and fight, and think you fight for me;
I wait but to reward your victory.

ABDALLA
But if I lose it, must I lose you too?

LYNDARAXA
You are too curious, if you more would know.
I know not what my future thoughts will be:
Poor women's thoughts are all extempore.
Wise men, indeed,
Beforehand a long chain of thoughts produce;
But ours are only for our present use.

ABDALLA

Those thoughts, you will not know, too well declare.
You mean to wait the final doom of war.

LYNDARAXA

I find you come to quarrel with me now;
Would you know more of me than I allow?
Whence are you grown that great divinity,
That with such ease into my thoughts can pry?
Indulgence does not with some tempers suit;
I see I must become more absolute.

ABDALLA

I must submit,
On what hard terms soe'er my peace be bought.

LYNDARAXA

Submit!—you speak as you were not in fault.—
'Tis evident the injury is mine;
For why should you my secret thoughts divine?

ABDALLA

Yet if we might be judged by reason's laws—

LYNDARAXA

Then you would have your reason judge my cause!—
Either confess your fault, or hold your tongue;
For I am sure I'm never in the wrong.

ABDALLA

Then I acknowledge it.

LYNDARAXA

Then I forgive.

ABDALLA

Under how hard a law poor lovers live!
Who, like the vanquished, must their right release,
And with the loss of reason buy their peace.—[Aside.
Madam, to show that you my power command,
I put my life and safety in your hand:—
Dispose of the Albayzyn as you please,
To your fair hands I here resign the keys.

LYNDARAXA

I take your gift, because your love it shows,
And faithful Selin for alcade chuse.

ABDALLA

Selin, from her alone your orders take.—
This one request, yet, madam, let me make,
That, from those turrets, you the assault will see;
And crown, once more, my arms with victory.

[Exeunt, leading her out.

[**SELIN** remains with **GAZUL** and **REDUAN**, his servants.

SELIN

Gazul, go tell my daughter that I wait—
You Reduan, bring the prisoner to his fate.

[Exeunt **GAZUL** and **REDUAN**.

Ere of my charge I will possession take,
A bloody sacrifice I mean to make:
The manes of my son shall smile this day,
While I, in blood, my vows of vengeance pay.

[Enter at one door **BENZAYDA**, with **GAZUL**; at the other, **OZMYN** bound, with **REDUAN**.

SELIN

I sent, Benzayda, to glad your eyes:
These rites we owe your brother's obsequies.—
You two [To **GAZUL** and **REDUAN**] the cursed Abencerrago bind:
You need no more to instruct you in my mind.

[They bind him to a corner of the stage.

BENZAYDA

In what sad object am I called to share?
Tell me, what is it, sir, you here prepare?

SELIN

'Tis what your dying brother did bequeath;
A scene of vengeance, and a pomp of death!

BENZAYDA

The horrid spectacle my soul does fright:
I want the heart to see the dismal sight.

SELIN

You are my principal invited guest,
Whose eyes I would not only feed, but feast:
You are to smile at his last groaning breath,

And laugh to see his eye-balls roll in death;
To judge the lingering soul's convulsive strife,
When thick short breath catches at parting life.

BENZAYDA
And of what marble do you think me made?

SELIN
What! can you be of just revenge afraid?

BENZAYDA
He killed my brother in his own defence.
Pity his youth, and spare his innocence.

SELIN
Art thou so soon to pardon murder won?
Can he be innocent, who killed my son?
Abenamar shall mourn as well as I;
His Ozmyn, for my Tarifa, shall die.
But since thou plead'st so boldly, I will see
That justice, thou would'st hinder, done by thee.
Here,

[Gives her his sword.]

— take the sword, and do a sister's part:
Pierce his, fond girl, or I will pierce thy heart.

OZMYN
To his commands I join my own request;
All wounds from you are welcome to my breast:
Think only, when your hand this act has done,
It has but finished what your eyes begun.
I thought, with silence, to have scorned my doom;
But now your noble pity has o'ercome;
Which I acknowledge with my latest breath,—
The first whoe'er began a love in death.

BENZAYDA [to SELIN]
Alas, what aid can my weak hand afford?
You see I tremble when I touch a sword:
The brightness dazzles me, and turns my sight;
Or, if I look, 'tis but to aim less right.

OZMYN
I'll guide the hand which must my death convey;
My leaping heart shall meet it half the way.

SELIN [to **BENZAYDA**]

Waste not the precious time in idle breath.

BENZAYDA

Let me resign this instrument of death.

[Giving the sword to her father, and then pulling it back.

Ah, no! I was too hasty to resign:
'Tis in your hand more mortal than in mine.

[Enter **HAMET**.

HAMET

The king is from the Alhambra beaten back,
And now preparing for a new attack;
To favour which, he wills, that instantly
You reinforce him with a new supply.

SELIN [to **BENZAYDA**

Think not, although my duty calls me hence,
That with the breach of yours I will dispense.
Ere my return, see my commands you do:
Let me find Ozmyn dead, and killed by you.—
Gazul and Reduan, attend her still;
And, if she dares to fail, perform my will.

[Exeunt **SELIN** and **HAMET**.

[**BENZAYDA** looks languishing on him, with her sword down; **GAZUL** and **REDUAN** standing
with drawn swords by her.

OZMYN

Defer not, fair Benzayda, my death:
Looking on you,
I should but live to sigh away my breath.
My eyes have done the work they had to do:
I take your image with me, which they drew;
And, when they close, I shall die full of you.

BENZAYDA

When parents their commands unjustly lay,
Children are privileged to disobey;
Yet from that breach of duty I am clear,
Since I submit the penalty to bear.
To die, or kill you, is the alternative;
Rather than take your life, I will not live.

OZMYN

This shows the excess of generosity;
But, madam, you have no pretence to die.
I should defame the Abencerrages race,
To let a lady suffer in my place.
But neither could that life, you would bestow,
Save mine; nor do you so much pity owe
To me, a stranger, and your house's foe.

BENZAYDA

From whencesoe'er their hate our houses drew,
I blush to tell you, I have none for you.
'Tis a confession which I should not make,
Had I more time to give, or you to take:
But, since death's near, and runs with so much force,
We must meet first, and intercept his course.

OZMYN

Oh, how unkind a comfort do you give!
Now I fear death again, and wish to live.
Life were worth taking, could I have it now;
But 'tis more good than heaven can e'er allow
To one man's portion, to have life and you.

BENZAYDA

Sure, at our births,
Death with our meeting planets danced above,
Or we were wounded by a mourning love!—

[Shouts within.

REDUAN

The noise returns, and doubles from behind;
It seems as if two adverse armies joined.—
Time presses us.

GAZUL

If longer you delay,
We must, though loth, your father's will obey.

OZMYN

Haste, madam, to fulfil his hard commands.
And rescue me from their ignoble hands.
Let me kiss yours, when you my wound begin,
Then easy death will slide with pleasure in.

BENZAYDA

Ah, gentle soldiers, some short time allow!

[To **GAZUL** and **REDUAN**.

My father has repented him ere now;
Or will repent him, when he finds me dead.
My clue of life is twined with Ozmyn's thread.

REDUAN
'Tis fatal to refuse her, or obey.—
But where is our excuse? what can we say?

BENZAYDA
Say any thing.
Say, that to kill the guiltless you were loth;
Or if you did, say, I would kill you both.

GAZUL
To disobey our orders is to die.—
I'll do't,—who dares oppose it?

REDUAN
That dare I.

[**REDUAN** stands before **OZMYN**, and fights with **GAZUL. BENZAYDA** unbinds **OZMYN**, and gives him her sword.

BENZAYDA
Stay not to see the issue of the fight;

[**REDUAN** kills **GAZUL.**

But haste to save yourself by speedy flight.

[**OZMYN** kneels to kiss her hand.

OZMYN
Did all mankind against my life conspire.
Without this blessing I would not retire.—
But madam, can I go and leave you here?
Your father's anger now for you I fear:
Consider you have done too much to stay.

BENZAYDA
Think not of me, but fly yourself away.

REDUAN
Haste quickly hence; the enemies are nigh!
From every part I see the soldiers fly.

The foes not only our assailants beat,
But fiercely sally out on their retreat,
And, like a sea broke loose, come on amain.

[Enter **ABENAMAR**, and a party with their swords drawn, driving in some of the enemies.

ABENAMAR
Traitors, you hope to save yourselves in vain!—
Your forfeit lives shall for your treason pay;
And Ozmyn's blood shall be revenged this day.

OZMYN
No, sir, your Ozmyn lives; and lives to own

[Kneeling to his father.

A father's piety to free his son.

ABENAMAR
My Ozmyn!—O, thou blessing of my age!

[Embracing him.

And art thou safe from their deluded rage!—
Whom must I praise for thy deliverance?
Was it thy valour, or the work of chance?

OZMYN
Nor chance, nor valour, could deliver me;
But 'twas a noble pity set me free.—
My liberty, and life,
And what your happiness you're pleased to call,
We to this charming beauty owe it all.

ABENAMAR
Instruct me, visible divinity!— [To her.
Instruct me by what name to worship thee!
For to thy virtue I would altars raise,
Since thou art much above all human praise.
But see,—

[Enter **ALMANZOR**, his sword bloody, leading in **ALMAHIDE** attended by **ESPERANZA**.

My other blessing, Almahide, is here!—
I'll to the king, and tell him she is near:
You, Ozmyn, on your fair deliverer wait,
And with your private joys the public celebrate.

[Exeunt **ABENAMAR**, **OZMYN** and **BENZAYDA**.

ALMANZOR

The work is done; now, madam, you are free;
At least, if I can give you liberty:
But you have chains which you yourself have chose;
And, O, that I could free you too from those!
But you are free from force, and have full power
To go, and kill my hopes and me, this hour.—
I see, then, you will go; but yet my toil
May he rewarded with a looking while.

ALMAHIDE

Almanzor can from every subject raise
New matter for our wonder and his praise.
You bound and freed me; but the difference is,
That showed your valour; but your virtue this.

ALMANZOR

Madam, you praise a funeral victory,
At whose sad pomp the conqueror must die.

ALMAHIDE

Conquest attends Almanzor every where;
I am too small a foe for him to fear:
But heroes still must be opposed by some,
Or they would want occasion to o'ercome.

ALMANZOR

Madam, I cannot on bare praises live:
Those, who abound in praises, seldom give.

ALMAHIDE

While I to all the world your worth make known,
May heaven reward the pity you have shown!

ALMANZOR

My love is languishing, and starved to death;
And would you give me charity—in breath?
Prayers are the alms of churchmen to the poor:
They send's to heaven, but drive us from their door.

ALMAHIDE

Cease, cease a suit
So vain to you, and troublesome to me,
If you will have me think that I am free.
If I am yet a slave, my bonds I'll bear;
But what I cannot grant, I will not hear.

ALMANZOR

You will not hear!—You must both hear and grant;
For, madam, there's an impudence in want.

ALMAHIDE

Your way is somewhat strange to ask relief
You ask with threatening, like a begging thief.—
Once more, Almanzor, tell me, am I free?

ALMANZOR

Madam, you are, from all the world,—but me!—
But as a pirate, when he frees the prize
He took from friends, sees the rich merchandize,
And, after he has freed it, justly buys;
So, when I have restored your liberty—
But then, alas, I am too poor to buy!

ALMAHIDE

Nay, now you use me just as pirates do:
You free me; but expect a ransom too.

ALMANZOR

You've all the freedom that a prince can have;
But greatness cannot be without a slave.
A monarch never can in private move,
But still is haunted with officious love.
So small an inconvenience you may bear;
'Tis all the fine fate sets upon the fair.

ALMAHIDE

Yet princes may retire, whene'er they please,
And breathe free air from out their palaces:
They go sometimes unknown, to shun their state;
And then, 'tis manners not to know or wait.

ALMANZOR

If not a subject then, a ghost I'll be;
And from a ghost, you know, no place is free.
Asleep, awake, I'll haunt you every where;
From my white shroud groan love into your ear:
When in your lover's arms you sleep at night,
I'll glide in cold betwixt, and seize my right:
And is't not better, in your nuptial bed,
To have a living lover than a dead?

ALMAHIDE

I can no longer bear to be accused,

As if what I could grant you, I refused.
My father's choice I never will dispute;
And he has chosen ere you moved your suit.
You know my case; if equal you can be,
Plead for yourself, and answer it for me.

ALMANZOR

Then, madam, in that hope you bid me live;
I ask no more than you may justly give:
But in strict justice there may favour be,
And may I hope that you have that for me?

ALMAHIDE

Why do you thus my secret thoughts pursue,
Which, known, hurt me, and cannot profit you?
Your knowledge but new troubles does prepare,
Like theirs who curious in their fortunes are.
To say, I could with more content be yours,
Tempts you to hope; but not that hope assures.
For since the king has right,
And favoured by my father in his suit,
It is a blossom which can bear no fruit.
Yet, if you dare attempt so hard a task,
May you succeed; you have my leave to ask.

ALMANZOR

I can with courage now my hopes pursue,
Since I no longer have to combat you.
That did the greatest difficulty bring;
The rest are small, a father and a king!

ALMAHIDE

Great souls discern not when the leap's too wide,
Because they only view the farther side.
Whatever you desire, you think is near;
But, with more reason, the event I fear.

ALMANZOR

No; there is a necessity in fate,
Why still the brave bold man is fortunate:
He keeps his object ever full in sight,
And that assurance holds him firm and right.
True, 'tis a narrow path that leads to bliss,
But right before there is no precipice:
Fear makes men look aside, and then their footing miss.

ALMAHIDE

I do your merit all the right I can;

Admiring virtue in a private man:
I only wish the king may grateful be,
And that my father with my eyes may see.
Might I not make it as my last request,—
Since humble carriage suits a suppliant best,—
That you would somewhat of your fierceness hide—
That inborn fire—I do not call it pride?

ALMANZOR
Born, as I am, still to command, not sue,
Yet you shall see that I can beg for you;
And if your father will require a crown,
Let him but name the kingdom, 'tis his own.
I am, but while I please, a private man;
I have that soul which empires first began.
From the dull crowd, which every king does lead,
I will pick out whom I will chuse to head:
The best and bravest souls I can select,
And on their conquered necks my throne erect.

[Exeunt.

ACT V

SCENE I

ABDALLA alone, under the walls of the Albayzyn.

ABDALLA
While she is mine, I have not yet lost all,
But in her arms shall have a gentle fall:
Blest in my love, although in war o'ercome,
I fly, like Antony from Actium,
To meet a better Cleopatra here.—
You of the watch! you of the watch! appear.

SOLDIER [above.]
Who calls below? What's your demand?

ABDALLA
'Tis I:
Open the gate with speed; the foe is nigh.

SOLDIER
What orders for admittance do you bring?

ABDALLA

Slave, my own orders; look, and know the king.

SOLDIER

I know you; but my charge is so severe,
That none, without exception, enter here.

ABDALLA

Traitor, and rebel! thou shalt shortly see
Thy orders are not to extend to me.

LYNDARAXA [above.]

What saucy slave so rudely does exclaim,
And brands my subject with a rebel's name?

ABDALLA

Dear Lyndaraxa, haste; the foes pursue.

LYNDARAXA

My lord, the Prince Abdalla, is it you?
I scarcely can believe the words I hear;
Could you so coarsely treat my officer?

ABDALLA

He forced me; but the danger nearer draws:
When I am entered, you shall know the cause.

LYNDARAXA

Entered! Why, have you any business here?

ABDALLA

I am pursued, the enemy is near.

LYNDARAXA

Are you pursued, and do you thus delay
To save yourself? Make haste, my lord, away.

ABDALLA

Give me not cause to think you mock my grief:
What place have I, but this, for my relief?

LYNDARAXA

This favour does your handmaid much oblige,
But we are not provided for a siege:
My subjects few; and their provision thin;
The foe is strong without, we weak within.
This to my noble lord may seem unkind,
But he will weigh it in his princely mind;

And pardon her, who does assurance want
So much, she blushes when she cannot grant.

ABDALLA
Yes, you may blush; and you have cause to weep.
Is this the faith you promised me to keep?
Ah yet, if to a lover you will bring
No succour, give your succour to a king.

LYNDARAXA
A king is he, whom nothing can withstand;
Who men and money can with ease command.
A king is he, whom fortune still does bless;
He is a king, who does a crown possess.
If you would have me think that you are he,
Produce to view your marks of sovereignty;
But if yourself alone for proof you bring,
You are but a single person, not a king.

ABDALLA
Ungrateful maid, did I for this rebel?
I say no more; but I have loved too well.

LYNDARAXA
Who but yourself did that rebellion move:
Did I e'er promise to receive your love?
Is it my fault you are not fortunate?
I love a king, but a poor rebel hate.

ABDALLA
Who follow fortune, still are in the right;
But let me be protected here this night.

LYNDARAXA
The place to-morrow will be circled round;
And then no way will for your flight be found.

ABDALLA
I hear my enemies just coming on;

[Trampling within.

Protect me but one hour, till they are gone.

LYNDARAXA
They'll know you have been here; it cannot be;
That very hour you stay, will ruin me:
For if the foe behold our interview,

I shall be thought a rebel too, like you.
Haste hence; and, that your flight may prosperous prove,
I'll recommend you to the powers above.

[Exit **LYNDARAXA** from above.

ABDALLA
She's gone: Ah, faithless and ungrateful maid!—
I hear some tread; and fear I am betrayed.
I'll to the Spanish king; and try if he,
To countenance his own right, will succour me:
There is more faith in Christian dogs, than thee.

[Exit.

[Enter **OZMYN, BENZAYDA,** and **ABENAMAR.**

BENZAYDA
I wish
(To merit all these thanks) I could have said,
My pity only did his virtue aid;
'Twas pity, but 'twas of a love-sick maid.
His manly suffering my esteem did move;
That bred compassion, and compassion love.

OZMYN
O blessing sold me at too cheap a rate!
My danger was the benefit of fate. [To his **FATHER.**
But that you may my fair deliverer know,
She was not only born our house's foe,
But to my death by powerful reasons led;
At least, in justice, she might wish me dead.

ABENAMAR
But why thus long do you her name conceal?

OZMYN
To gain belief for what I now reveal:
Even thus prepared, you scarce can think it true,
The saver of my life from Selin drew
Her birth; and was his sister whom I slew.

ABENAMAR
No more; it cannot, was not, must not be:
Upon my blessing, say not it was she.
The daughter of the only man I hate!
Two contradictions twisted in a fate!

OZMYN

The mutual hate, which you and Selin bore,
Does but exalt her generous pity more.
Could she a brother's death forgive to me,
And cannot you forget her family?
Can you so ill requite the life I owe,
To reckon her, who gave it, still your foe?
It lends too great a lustre to her line,
To let her virtue ours so much out-shine.

ABENAMAR

Thou gav'st her line the advantage which they have,
By meanly taking of the life they gave.
Grant that it did in her a pity shew;
But would my son be pitied by a foe?
She has the glory of thy act defaced:
Thou kill'dst her brother; but she triumphs last:
Poorly for us our enmity would cease;
When we are beaten, we receive a peace.

BENZAYDA

If that be all in which you disagree,
I must confess 'twas Ozmyn conquered me.
Had I beheld him basely beg his life,
I should not now submit to be his wife;
But when I saw his courage death controul,
I paid a secret homage to his soul;
And thought my cruel father much to blame,
Since Ozmyn's virtue his revenge did shame.

ABENAMAR

What constancy can'st thou e'er hope to find
In that unstable, and soon conquered mind?
What piety can'st thou expect from her,
Who could forgive a brother's murderer?
Or, what obedience hop'st thou to be paid,
From one who first her father disobeyed?

OZMYN

Nature, that bids us parents to obey,
Bids parents their commands by reason weigh;
And you her virtue by your praise did own,
Before you knew by whom the act was done.

ABENAMAR

Your reasons speak too much of insolence;
Her birth's a crime past pardon or defence.
Know, that as Selin was not won by thee,

Neither will I by Selin's daughter be.
Leave her, or cease henceforth to be my son:
This is my will; and this I will have done.

[Exit **ABENAMAR**.

OZMYN
It is a murdering will,
That whirls along with an impetuous sway,
And, like chain-shot, sweeps all things in its way.
He does my honour want of duty call;
To that, and love, he has no right at all.

BENZAYDA
No, Ozmyn, no; it is a much less ill
To leave me, than dispute a father's will:
If I had any title to your love,
Your father's greater right does mine remove:
Your vows and faith I give you back again,
Since neither can be kept without a sin.

OZMYN
Nothing but death my vows can give me back:
They are not yours to give, nor mine to take.

BENZAYDA
Nay, think not, though I could your vows resign,
My love or virtue could dispense with mine.
I would extinguish your unlucky fire,
To make you happy in some new desire:
I can preserve enough for me and you,
And love, and be unfortunate, for two.

OZMYN
In all that's good and great
You vanquish me so fast, that in the end
I shall have nothing left me to defend.
From every post you force me to remove;
But let me keep my last entrenchment, love.

BENZAYDA
Love then, my Ozmyn; I will be content

[Giving her hand.

To make you wretched by your own consent:
Live poor, despised, and banished for my sake,
And all the burden of my sorrows take;

For, as for me, in whatsoe'er estate,
While I have you, I must be fortunate.

OZMYN
Thus then, secured of what we hold most dear,
(Each other's love) we'll go—I know not where.
For where, alas, should we our flight begin?
The foe's without; our parents are within.

BENZAYDA
I'll fly to you, and you shall fly to me;
Our flight but to each other's arms shall be.
To providence and chance permit the rest;
Let us but love enough, and we are blest.

[Exeunt.

SCENE II

Enter **BOABDELIN, ABENAMAR, ABDELMELECH, GUARDS, ZULEMA** and **HAMET**, Prisoners.

ABDELMELECH
They are Lyndaraxa's brothers; for her sake,
Their lives and pardon my request I make.

BOABDELIN
Then, Zulema and Hamet, live; but know,
Your lives to Abdelmelech's suit you owe.

ZULEMA
The grace received so much my hope exceeds,
That words come weak and short to answer deeds.
You've made a venture, sir, and time must shew,
If this great mercy you did well bestow.

BOABDELIN
You, Abdelmelech, haste before 'tis night,
And close pursue my brother in his flight.

[Exeunt **ABDELMELECH, ZULEMA,** and **HAMET.**

[Enter **ALMANZOR, ALMAHIDE,** and **ESPERANZA.**

But see, with Almahide
The brave Almanzor comes, whose conquering sword
The crown, it once took from me, has restored.

How can I recompence so great desert!

ALMANZOR

I bring you, sir, performed in every part,
My promise made; your foes are fled or slain;
Without a rival, absolute you reign.
Yet though, in justice, this enough may be,
It is too little to be done by me:
I beg to go,
Where my own courage and your fortune calls,
To chase these misbelievers from our walls.
I cannot breathe within this narrow space;
My heart's too big, and swells beyond the place.

BOABDELIN

You can perform, brave warrior, what you please;
Fate listens to your voice, and then decrees.
Now I no longer fear the Spanish powers;
Already we are free, and conquerors.

ALMANZOR

Accept, great king, to-morrow, from my hand,
The captive head of conquered Ferdinand.
You shall not only what you lost regain,
But o'er the Biscayan mountains to the main,
Extend your sway, where never Moor did reign.

ABENAMAR

What, in another, vanity would seem,
Appears but noble confidence in him;
No haughty boasting, but a manly pride;
A soul too fiery, and too great to guide:
He moves excentric, like a wandering star,
Whose motion's just, though 'tis not regular.

BOABDELIN

It is for you, brave man, and only you,
Greatly to speak, and yet more greatly do.
But, if your benefits too far extend,
I must be left ungrateful in the end:
Yet somewhat I would pay,
Before my debts above all reckoning grow,
To keep me from the shame of what I owe.
But you
Are conscious to yourself of such desert,
That of your gift I fear to offer part.

ALMANZOR

When I shall have declared my high request,
So much presumption there will be confest,
That you will find your gifts I do not shun;
But rather much o'er-rate the service done.

BOABDELIN
Give wing to your desires, and let 'em fly,
Secure they cannot mount a pitch too high.
So bless me, Alha, both in peace and war,
As I accord, whate'er your wishes are.

ALMANZOR
Emboldened by the promise of a prince,

[Putting one knee to the ground.

I ask this lady now with confidence.

BOABDELIN
You ask the only thing I cannot grant.

[The **KING** and **ABENAMAR** look amazedly on each other.

But, as a stranger, you are ignorant
Of what by public fame my subjects know;
She is my mistress.

ABENAMAR
—And my daughter too.

ALMANZOR
Believe, old man, that I her father knew:
What else should make Almanzor kneel to you?—
Nor doubt, sir, but your right to her was known:
For had you had no claim but love alone,
I could produce a better of my own.

ALMAHIDE [softly to him.]
Almanzor, you forget my last request:
Your words have too much haughtiness expressed.
Is this the humble way you were to move?

ALMANZOR [to her.]
I was too far transported by my love.
Forgive me; for I had not learned to sue
To any thing before, but heaven and you.—
Sir, at your feet, I make it my request—[To the **KING**.

[First line kneeling: second, rising, and boldly.

Though, without boasting, I deserve her best;
For you her love with gaudy titles sought,
But I her heart with blood and dangers bought.

BOABDELIN
The blood, which you have shed in her defence,
Shall have in time a fitting recompence:
Or, if you think your services delayed,
Name but your price, and you shall soon be paid.

ALMANZOR
My price!—why, king, you do not think you deal
With one who sets his services to sale?
Reserve your gifts for those who gifts regard;
And know, I think myself above reward.

BOABDELIN
Then sure you are some godhead; and our care
Must be to come with incense and with prayer.

ALMANZOR
As little as you think yourself obliged,
You would be glad to do't, when next besieged.
But I am pleased there should be nothing due;
For what I did was for myself, not you.

BOABDELIN
You with contempt on meaner gifts look down;
And, aiming at my queen, disdain my crown.
That crown, restored, deserves no recompence.
Since you would rob the fairest jewel thence.
Dare not henceforth ungrateful me to call;
Whate'er I owed you, this has cancelled all.

ALMANZOR
I'll call thee thankless, king, and perjured both:
Thou swor'st by Alha, and hast broke thy oath.
But thou dost well; thou tak'st the cheapest way;
Not to own services thou canst not pay.

BOABDELIN
My patience more than pays thy service past;
But now this insolence shall be thy last.
Hence from my sight! and take it as a grace,
Thou liv'st, and art but banished from the place.

ALMANZOR
Where'er I go, there can no exile be;
But from Almanzor's sight I banish thee:
I will not now, if thou wouldst beg me, stay;
But I will take my Almahide away.
Stay thou with all thy subjects here; but know,
We leave thy city empty when we go.

[Takes **ALMAHIDE'S** hand.

BOABDELIN
Fall on; take; kill the traitor.

[The **GUARDS** fall on him; he makes at the KING through the midst of them, and falls upon him; they disarm him, and rescue the King.

ALMANZOR
—Base and poor,
Blush that thou art Almanzor's conqueror.
[**ALMAHIDE** wrings her hands, then turns and veils her face.

Farewell, my Almahide!
Life of itself will go, now thou art gone,
Like flies in winter, when they lose the sun.

[**ABENAMAR** whispers the **KING** a little, then speaks aloud.

ABENAMAR
Revenge, and taken so secure a way,
Are blessings which heaven sends not every day.

BOABDELIN
I will at leisure now revenge my wrong;
And, traitor, thou shalt feel my vengeance long:
Thou shalt not die just at thy own desire,
But see my nuptials, and with rage expire.

ALMANZOR
Thou darest not marry her while I'm in sight:
With a bent brow thy priest and thee I'll fright;
And in that scene,
Which all thy hopes and wishes should content,
The thought of me shall make thee impotent.

[He is led off by **GUARDS**.

BOABDELIN
As some fair tulip, by a storm oppressed, [To **ALMAHIDE**.

Shrinks up, and folds its silken arms to rest;
And, bending to the blast, all pale and dead,
Hears, from within, the wind sing round its head,—
So, shrouded up, your beauty disappears:
Unveil, my love, and lay aside your fears.
The storm, that caused your fright, is passed and done.

[**ALMAHIDE** unveiling, and looking round for **ALMANZOR**.

ALMAHIDE
So flowers peep out too soon, and miss the sun.

[Turning from him.

BOABDELIN
What mystery in this strange behaviour lies?

ALMAHIDE
Let me for ever hide these guilty eyes,
Which lighted my Almanzor to his tomb;
Or, let them blaze, to show me there a room.

BOABDELIN
Heaven lent their lustre for a nobler end;
A thousand torches must their light attend,
To lead you to a temple and a crown.
Why does my fairest Almahide frown?
Am I less pleasing then I was before,
Or, is the insolent Almanzor more?

ALMAHIDE
I justly own that I some pity have,
Not for the insolent, but for the brave.

ABENAMAR
Though to your king your duty you neglect,
Know, Almahide, I look for more respect:
And, if a parent's charge your mind can move,
Receive the blessing of a monarch's love.

ALMAHIDE
Did he my freedom to his life prefer,
And shall I wed Almanzor's murderer?
No, sir; I cannot to your will submit;
Your way's too rugged for my tender feet.

ABENAMAR
You must be driven where you refuse to go;

And taught, by force, your happiness to know.

ALMAHIDE
To force me, sir, is much unworthy you,

[Smiling scornfully.

And, when you would, impossible to do.
If force could bend me, you might think, with shame,
That I debase the blood from whence I came.
My soul is soft, which you may gently lay
In your loose palm; but, when 'tis pressed to stay,
Like water, it deludes your grasp, and slips away.

BOABDELIN
I find I must revoke what I decreed:
Almanzor's death my nuptials must precede.
Love is a magic which the lover ties;
But charms still end when the magician dies.
Go; let me hear my hated rival's dead; [To his **GUARD**.
And, to convince my eyes, bring back his head.

ALMAHIDE
Go on: I wish no other way to prove
That I am worthy of Almanzor's love.
We will in death, at least, united be:
I'll shew you I can die as well as he.

BOABDELIN
What should I do! when equally I dread
Almanzor living and Almanzor dead!—
Yet, by your promise, you are mine alone.

ALMAHIDE
How dare you claim my faith, and break your own?

ABENAMAR
This for your virtue is a weak defence:
No second vows can with your first dispense.
Yet, since the king did to Almanzor swear,
And in his death ungrateful may appear,
He ought, in justice, first to spare his life,
And then to claim your promise as his wife.

ALMAHIDE
Whate'er my secret inclinations be,
To this, since honour ties me, I agree:
Yet I declare, and to the world will own,

That, far from seeking, I would shun the throne.
And with Almanzor lead a humble life:
There is a private greatness in his wife.

BOABDELIN
That little love I have, I hardly buy;
You give my rival all, while you deny:
Yet, Almahide, to let you see your power,
Your loved Almanzor shall be free this hour.
You are obeyed; but 'tis so great a grace,
That I could wish me in my rival's place.

[Exeunt **KING** and **ABENAMAR**.

ALMAHIDE
How blessed was I before this fatal day,
When all I knew of love, was to obey!
'Twas life becalmed, without a gentle breath;
Though not so cold, yet motionless as death.
A heavy quiet state; but love, all strife,
All rapid, is the hurricane of life.
Had love not shewn me, I had never seen
An excellence beyond Boabdelin.
I had not, aiming higher, lost my rest;
But with a vulgar good been dully blest:
But, in Almanzor, having seen what's rare,
Now I have learnt too sharply to compare;
And, like a favourite quickly in disgrace,
Just knew the value ere I lost the place.

[To her **ALMANZOR**, bound and guarded.

ALMANZOR
I see the end for which I'm hither sent,
To double, by your sight, my punishment.
There is a shame in bonds I cannot bear;
Far more than death, to meet your eyes I fear.

ALMAHIDE
That shame of long continuance shall not be:

[Unbinding him.

The king, at my entreaty, sets you free.

ALMANZOR
The king! my wonder's greater than before;
How did he dare my freedom to restore?

He like some captive lion uses me;
He runs away before he sets me free,
And takes a sanctuary in his court:
I'll rather lose my life than thank him for't.

ALMAHIDE
If any subject for your thanks there be,
The king expects them not, you owe them me.
Our freedoms through each other's hands have past;
You give me my revenge in winning last.

ALMANZOR
Then fate commodiously for me has done;
To lose mine there where I would have it won.

ALMAHIDE
Almanzor, you too soon will understand,
That what I win is on another's hand.
The king (who doomed you to a cruel fate)
Gave to my prayers both his revenge and hate;
But at no other price would rate your life,
Than my consent and oath to be his wife.

ALMANZOR
Would you, to save my life, my love betray?
Here; take me; bind me; carry me away;
Kill me! I'll kill you if you disobey. [To the **GUARDS**.

ALMAHIDE
That absolute command your love does give,
I take, and charge you by that power to live.

ALMANZOR
When death, the last of comforts, you refuse,
Your power, like heaven upon the damned, you use;
You force me in my being to remain,
To make me last, and keep me fresh for pain.
When all my joys are gone,
What cause can I for living longer give,
But a dull, lazy habitude to live?

ALMAHIDE
Rash men, like you, and impotent of will,
Give chance no time to turn, but urge her still;
She would repent; you push the quarrel on,
And once because she went, she must be gone.

ALMANZOR

She shall not turn; what is it she can do,
To recompense me for the loss of you?

ALMAHIDE
Heaven will reward your worth some better way:
At least, for me, you have but lost one day.
Nor is't a real loss which you deplore;
You sought a heart that was engaged before.
'Twas a swift love which took you in his way;
Flew only through your heart, but made no stay:
'Twas but a dream, where truth had not a place;
A scene of fancy, moved so swift a pace,
And shifted, that you can but think it was;—
Let then, the short vexatious vision pass.

ALMANZOR
My joys, indeed, are dreams; but not my pain:
'Twas a swift ruin, but the marks remain.
When some fierce fire lays goodly buildings waste,
Would you conclude
There had been none, because the burning's past?

ALMAHIDE
It was your fault that fire seized all your breast;
You should have blown up some to save the rest:
But 'tis, at worst, but so consumed by fire,
As cities are, that by their fall rise higher.
Build love a nobler temple in my place;
You'll find the fire has but enlarged your space.

ALMANZOR
Love has undone me; I am grown so poor,
I sadly view the ground I had before,
But want a stock, and ne'er can build it more.

ALMAHIDE
Then say what charity I can allow;
I would contribute if I knew but how.
Take friendship; or, if that too small appear,
Take love,—which sisters may to brothers bear.

ALMANZOR
A sister's love! that is so palled a thing,
What pleasure can it to a lover bring?
'Tis like thin food to men in fevers spent;
Just keeps alive, but gives no nourishment.
What hopes, what fears, what transports can it move?
'Tis but the ghost of a departed love.

ALMAHIDE

You, like some greedy cormorant, devour
All my whole life can give you in an hour.
What more I can do for you is to die,
And that must follow, if you this deny.
Since I gave up my love, that you might live,
You, in refusing life, my sentence give.

ALMANZOR

Far from my breast be such an impious thought!
Your death would lose the quiet mine had sought.
I'll live for you, in spite of misery;
But you shall grant that I had rather die.
I'll be so wretched, filled with such despair,
That you shall see, to live was more to dare.

ALMAHIDE

Adieu, then, O my soul's far better part!
Your image sticks so close,
That the blood follows from my rending heart.
A last farewell!
For, since a last must come, the rest are vain,
Like gasps in death, which but prolong our pain.
But, since the king is now a part of me,
Cease from henceforth to be his enemy.
Go now, for pity go! for, if you stay,
I fear I shall have something still to say.
Thus—I for ever shut you from my sight.

[Veils.

ALMANZOR

Like one thrust out in a cold winters night,
Yet shivering underneath your gate I stay;
One look—I cannot go before 'tis day.—

[She beckons him to be gone.

Not one—Farewell: Whate'er my sufferings be
Within, I'll speak farewell as loud as she:
I will not be out-done in constancy.—

[She turns her back.

Then like a dying conqueror I go;
At least I have looked last upon my foe.
I go—but, if too heavily I move,

I walk encumbered with a weight of love.
Fain I would leave the thought of you behind,
But still, the more I cast you from my mind,
You dash, like water, back, when thrown against the wind.

[Exit.

[As he goes off, the **KING** meets him with **ABENAMAR**; they stare at each other without saluting.

BOABDELIN
With him go all my fears: A guard there wait,
And see him safe without the city gate.

[To them **ABDELMELECH**.

Now, Abdelmelech, is my brother dead?

ABDELMELECH
Th' usurper to the Christian camp is fled;
Whom as Granada's lawful king they own,
And vow, by force, to seat him on the throne.
Mean time the rebels in the Albayzyn rest;
Which is in Lyndaraxa's name possest.

BOABDELIN
Haste and reduce it instantly by force.

ABDELMELECH
First give me leave to prove a milder course.
She will, perhaps, on summons yield the place.

BOABDELIN
We cannot to your suit refuse her grace.

[One enters hastily, and whispers **ABENAMAR**.

ABENAMAR
How fortune persecutes this hoary head!
My Ozmyn is with Selin's daughter fled.
But he's no more my son:
My hate shall like a Zegry him pursue,
'Till I take back what blood from me he drew.

BOABDELIN
Let war and vengeance be to-morrow's care;
But let us to the temple now repair.
A thousand torches make the mosque more bright:
This must be mine and Almahide's night.

Hence, ye importunate affairs of state,
You should not tyrannize on love, but wait.
Had life no love, none would for business live;
Yet still from love the largest part we give;
And must be forced, in empire's weary toil,
To live long wretched, to be pleased a while.

[Exeunt.

EPILOGUE

Success, which can no more than beauty last,
Makes our sad poet mourn your favours past:
For, since without desert he got a name,
He fears to lose it now with greater shame.
Fame, like a little mistress of the town,
Is gained with ease, but then she's lost as soon:
For, as those tawdry misses, soon or late,
Jilt such as keep them at the highest rate;
And oft the lacquey, or the brawny clown,
Gets what is hid in the loose-bodied gown,—
So, fame is false to all that keep her long;
And turns up to the fop that's brisk and young.
Some wiser poet now would leave fame first;
But elder wits are, like old lovers, cursed:
Who, when the vigour of their youth is spent,
Still grow more fond, as they grow impotent.
This, some years hence, our poet's case may prove;
But yet, he hopes, he's young enough to love.
When forty comes, if e'er he live to see
That wretched, fumbling age of poetry,
'Twill be high time to bid his muse adieu:—
Well may he please himself, but never you.
Till then, he'll do as well as he began,
And hopes you will not find him less a man.
Think him not duller for this year's delay;
He was prepared, the women were away;
And men, without their parts, can hardly play.
If they, through sickness, seldom did appear,
Pity the virgins of each theatre:
For, at both houses, 'twas a sickly year!
And pity us, your servants, to whose cost,
In one such sickness, nine whole months are lost.
Their stay, he fears, has ruined what he writ:
Long waiting both disables love and wit.
They thought they gave him leisure to do well;
But, when they forced him to attend, he fell!

Yet, though he much has failed, he begs, to-day,
You will excuse his unperforming play:
Weakness sometimes great passion does express;
He had pleased better, had he loved you less.

Whether heroic verse ought to be admitted into serious plays, is not now to be disputed: it is already in possession of the stage, and I dare confidently affirm, that very few tragedies, in this age, shall be received without it. All the arguments which are formed against it, can amount to no more than this, that it is not so near conversation as prose, and therefore not so natural. But it is very clear to all who understand poetry, that serious plays ought not to imitate conversation too nearly. If nothing were to be raised above that level, the foundation of poetry would be destroyed. And if you once admit of a latitude, that thoughts may be exalted, and that images and actions may be raised above the life, and described in measure without rhyme, that leads you insensibly from your own principles to mine: you are already so far onward of your way, that you have forsaken the imitation of ordinary converse. You are gone beyond it; and to continue where you are, is to lodge in the open fields, betwixt two inns. You have lost that which you call natural, and have not acquired the last perfection of art. But it was only custom which cozened us so long; we thought, because Shakespeare and Fletcher went no farther, that there the pillars of poetry were to be erected; that, because they excellently described passion without rhyme, therefore rhyme was not capable of describing it. But time has now convinced most men of that error. It is indeed so difficult to write verse, that the adversaries of it have a good plea against many, who undertook that task, without being formed by art or nature for it. Yet, even they who have written worst in it, would have written worse without it: They have cozened many with their sound, who never took the pains to examine their sense. In fine, they have succeeded; though, it is true, they have more dishonoured rhyme by their good success, than they have done by their ill. But I am willing to let fall this argument: It is free for every man to write, or not to write, in verse, as he judges it to be, or not to be, his talent; or as he imagines the audience will receive it.

For heroic plays, in which only I have used it without the mixture of prose, the first light we had of them, on the English theatre, was from the late Sir William D'Avenant. It being forbidden him in the rebellious times to act tragedies and comedies, because they contained some matter of scandal to those good people, who could more easily dispossess their lawful sovereign, than endure a wanton jest, he was forced to turn his thoughts another way, and to introduce the examples of moral virtue, writ in verse, and performed in recitative music. The original of this music, and of the scenes which adorned his work, he had from the Italian operas; but he heightened his characters, as I may probably imagine, from the example of Corneille and some French poets. In this condition did this part of poetry remain at his majesty's return; when, growing bolder, as being now owned by a public authority, he reviewed his "Siege of Rhodes," and caused it be acted as a just drama. But as few men have the happiness to begin and finish any new project, so neither did he live to make his design perfect: There wanted the fulness of a plot, and the variety of characters to form it as it ought; and, perhaps, something might have been added to the beauty of the style. All which he would have performed with more exactness, had he pleased to have given us another work of the same nature. For myself and others, who come after him, we are bound, with all veneration to his memory, to acknowledge what advantage we received from that excellent groundwork which he laid: And, since it is an easy thing to add to what already is invented, we ought all of us, without envy to him, or partiality to ourselves, to yield him the precedence in it.

Having done him this justice, as my guide, I may do myself so much, as to give an account of what I have performed after him. I observed then, as I said, what was wanting to the perfection of his "Siege of Rhodes;" which was design, and variety of characters. And in the midst of this consideration by mere accident, I opened the next book that lay by me, which was "Ariosto," in Italian; and the very first two lines of that poem gave me light to all I could desire;

Le donne, i cavalier, l'arme, gli amori,
Le cortesie, l'audaci imprese io canto, &c.

For the very next reflection which I made was this, that an heroic play ought to be an imitation, in little, of an heroic poem; and, consequently, that love and valour ought to be the subject of it. Both these Sir William D'Avenant had begun to shadow; but it was so, as first discoverers draw their maps, with headlands, and promontories, and some few outlines of somewhat taken at a distance, and which the designer saw not clearly. The common drama obliged him to a plot well formed and pleasant, or, as the ancients call it, one entire and great action. But this he afforded not himself in a story, which he neither filled with persons, nor beautified with characters, nor varied with accidents. The laws of an heroic poem did not dispense with those of the other, but raised them to a greater height, and indulged him a farther liberty of fancy, and of drawing all things as far above the ordinary proportion of the stage, as that is beyond the common words and actions of human life; and, therefore, in the scanting of his images and design, he complied not enough with the greatness and majesty of an heroic poem.

I am sorry I cannot discover my opinion of this kind of writing, without dissenting much from his, whose memory I love and honour. But I will do it with the same respect to him, as if he were now alive, and overlooking my paper while I write. His judgment of an heroic poem was this: "That it ought to be dressed in a more familiar and easy shape; more fitted to the common actions and passions of human life; and, in short, more like a glass of nature, shewing us ourselves in our ordinary habits and figuring a more practicable virtue to us, than was done by the ancients or moderns." Thus he takes the image of an heroic poem from the drama, or stage poetry; and accordingly intended to divide it into five books, representing the same number of acts; and every book into several cantos, imitating the scenes which compose our acts.

But this, I think, is rather a play in narration, as I may call it, than an heroic poem. If at least you will not prefer the opinion of a single man to the practice of the most excellent authors, both of ancient and latter ages. I am no admirer of quotations; but you shall hear, if you please, one of the ancients delivering his judgment on this question; it is Petronius Arbiter, the most elegant, and one of the most judicious authors of the Latin tongue; who, after he had given many admirable rules for the structure and beauties of an epic poem, concludes all in these following words:—

"Non enim res gestæ versibus comprehendendæ sunt, quod longe melius historici faciunt: sed, per ambages deorumque ministeria, præcipitanaus est liber spiritus, ut potius furentis animi vaticinatio appareat, quam religiosæ orationis, sub testibus, fides."

In which sentence, and his own essay of a poem, which immediately he gives you, it is thought he taxes Lucan, who followed too much the truth of history, crowded sentences together, was too full of points, and too often offered at somewhat which had more of the sting of an epigram, than of the dignity and state of an heroic poem. Lucan used not much the help of his heathen deities: There was neither the ministry of the gods, nor the precipitation of the soul, nor the fury of a prophet (of which my author speaks), in his Pharsalia; he treats you more like a philosopher than a poet, and instructs you in verse, with what he had been taught by his uncle Seneca in prose. In one word, he walks soberly afoot, when he might fly. Yet Lucan is not always this religious historian. The oracle of Appius and the witchcraft of Erictho, will somewhat atone for him, who was, indeed, bound up by an ill-chosen and known argument, to follow truth with great exactness. For my part, I am of opinion, that neither Homer, Virgil, Statius, Ariosto, Tasso, nor our English Spencer, could have formed their poems half so beautiful, without those gods and spirits, and those enthusiastic parts of poetry, which compose the most noble parts of all their writings. And I will ask any man who loves heroic poetry (for I will not dispute their tastes who do not), if the ghost of Polydorus in Virgil, the Enchanted Wood in Tasso, and the Bower of Bliss in Spencer (which he borrows from that admirable Italian) could have been omitted, without taking from their works some of the greatest beauties in them. And if any man object the improbabilities of a spirit appearing, or of a palace raised by magic; I boldly answer him, that an heroic poet is not tied to a bare representation of what is true, or exceeding probable; but that he may let himself loose to visionary objects and to the representation of such things, as, depending not on sense, and therefore not to be comprehended by knowledge, may give him a freer scope for imagination. It is enough that, in all ages and religions, the greatest part of mankind have believed the power of magic, and that there are spirits or spectres which have appeared. This, I say, is foundation enough for poetry; and I dare farther affirm, that the whole doctrine of separated beings, whether those spirits are incorporeal substances, (which Mr Hobbes, with some reason, thinks to imply a contradiction) or that they are a thinner and more aërial sort of bodies, (as some of the fathers have conjectured) may better be explicated by poets than by philosophers or divines. For their speculations on this subject are wholly poetical; they have only their fancy for their guide; and that, being sharper in an excellent poet, than it is likely it should in a phlegmatic, heavy gownman, will see farther in its own empire, and produce more satisfactory notions on those dark and doubtful problems.

Some men think they have raised a great argument against the use of spectres and magic in heroic poetry, by saying they are unnatural; but whether they or I believe there are such things, is not material; it is enough that, for aught we know, they may be in nature; and whatever is, or may be, is not properly unnatural. Neither am I much concerned at Mr Cowley's verses before "Gondibert," though his authority is almost sacred to me: It is true, he has resembled the old epic poetry to a fantastic fairy-land; but he has contradicted himself by his own example: For he has himself made use of angels and visions in his "Davideis," as well as Tasso in his "Godfrey."

What I have written on this subject will not be thought a digression by the reader, if he please to remember what I said in the beginning of this essay, that I have modelled my heroic plays by the rules of an heroic poem. And if that be the most noble, the most pleasant, and the most instructive way of writing in verse, and withal the highest pattern of human life, as all poets have agreed, I shall need no other argument to justify my choice in this imitation. One advantage the drama has above the other, namely, that it represents to view what the poem only does relate; and, Segnius irritant animum demissa per aures, quam quæ sunt oculis subjecta fidelibus, as Horace tells us.

To those who object my frequent use of drums and trumpets, and my representations of battles, I answer, I introduced them not on the English stage: Shakespeare used them frequently; and though Jonson shews no battle in his "Catiline," yet you hear from behind the scenes the sounding of trumpets, and the shouts of fighting armies. But, I add farther, that these warlike instruments, and even their presentations of fighting on the stage, are no more than necessary to produce the effects of an heroic play; that is, to raise the imagination of the audience and to persuade them, for the time, that what they behold on the theatre is really performed. The poet is then to endeavour an absolute dominion over the minds of the spectators; for, though our fancy will contribute to its own deceit, yet a writer ought to help its operation: And that the Red Bull has formerly done the same, is no more an argument against our practice, than it would be for a physician to forbear an approved medicine, because a mountebank has used it with success.

Thus I have given a short account of heroic plays. I might now, with the usual eagerness of an author, make a particular defence of this. But the common opinion (how unjust soever) has been so much to my advantage, that I have reason to be satisfied, and to suffer with patience all that can be urged against it.

For, otherwise, what can be more easy for me, than to defend the character of Almanzor, which is one great exception that is made against the play? 'Tis said, that Almanzor is no perfect pattern of heroic virtue, that he is a contemner of kings, and that he is made to perform impossibilities.

I must therefore avow, in the first place, from whence I took the character. The first image I had of him, was from the Achilles of Homer; the next from Tasso's Rinaldo, (who was a copy of the former) and the third from the Artaban of Monsieur Calpranede, who has imitated both. The original of these, Achilles, is taken by Homer for his hero; and is described by him as one, who in strength and courage surpassed the rest of the Grecian army; but, withal, of so fiery a temper, so impatient of an injury, even from his king and general, that when his mistress was to be forced from him by the command of Agamemnon, he not only disobeyed it, but returned him an answer full of contumely, and in the most opprobrious terms he could imagine; they are Homer's words which follow, and I have cited but some few amongst a multitude.

[Greek: Oinobares, kynos ommat' echôn, kradiên d' elaphoio.]
—Il. a. v. 225.

[Greek: Dêmoboros basileus,] &c. —Il. a. v. 231.

Nay, he proceeded so far in his insolence, as to draw out his sword, with intention to kill him;

[Greek: Elketo d' ek koleoio mega xiphos.]
—Il. a. v. 194.

and, if Minerva had not appeared, and held his hand, he had executed his design; and it was all she could do to dissuade him from it. The event was, that he left the army, and would fight no more. Agamemnon gives his character thus to Nestor;

[Greek: All' hod' anêr ethelei peri pantôn emmenai allôn,
Pantôn men krateein ethelei, pantessi d' anassein.]
—Il. a. v. 287, 288

and Horace gives the same description of him in his Art of Poetry.

—Honoratum si fortè reponis Achillem,
Inpiger, iracundus, inexorabilis, acer,
Jura neget sibi nata, nihil non arroget armis.

Tasso's chief character, Rinaldo, was a man of the same temper; for, when he had slain Gernando in his heat of passion, he not only refused to be judged by Godfrey, his general, but threatened that if he came to seize him, he would right himself by arms upon him; witness these following lines of Tasso:

Venga egli, o mundi, io terrò fermo il piede:
Giudici fian tra noi la sorte, e l'arme;
Fera tragedia vuol che s'appresenti,
Per lor diporto, alle nemiche genti.

You see how little these great authors did esteem the point of honour, so much magnified by the French, and so ridiculously aped by us. They made their heroes men of honour; but so, as not to divest them quite of human passions and frailties: they content themselves to shew you, what men of great spirits would certainly do when they were provoked, not what they were obliged to do by the strict rules of moral virtue. For my own part, I declare myself for Homer and Tasso, and am more in love with Achilles and Rinaldo, than with Cyrus and Oroondates. I shall never subject my characters to the French standard, where love and honour are to be weighed by drams and scruples: Yet, where I have designed the patterns of exact virtues, such as in this play are the parts of Almahide, of Ozmyn, and Benzayda, I may safely challenge the best of theirs.

But Almanzor is taxed with changing sides: and what tie has he on him to the contrary? He is not born their subject whom he serves, and he is injured by them to a very high degree. He threatens them, and speaks insolently of sovereign power; but so do Achilles and Rinaldo, who were subjects and soldiers to Agamemnon and Godfrey of Bulloigne. He talks extravagantly in his passion; but, if I would take the pains to quote an hundred passages of Ben Jonson's Cethegus, I could easily shew you, that the rhodomontades of Almanzor are neither so irrational as his, nor so impossible to be put in execution; for Cethegus threatens to destroy nature, and to raise a new one out of it; to kill all the senate for his part of the action; to look Cato dead; and a thousand other things as extravagant he says, but performs not one action in the play.

But none of the former calumnies will stick; and, therefore, it is at last charged upon me, that Almanzor does all things; or if you will have an absurd accusation, in their nonsense who make it, that he performs impossibilities: they say, that being a stranger, he appeases two fighting factions, when the authority of their lawful sovereign could not. This is indeed the most improbable of all his actions, but it is far from being impossible. Their king had made himself contemptible to his people, as the history of Granada tells us; and Almanzor, though a stranger, yet was already known to them by his gallantry in the Juego de torros, his engagement on the weaker side, and more especially by the character of his person and brave actions, given by Abdalla just before; and, after all, the greatness of the enterprise consisted only in the daring, for he had the king's guards to second him: But we have read both of Cæsar, and many other generals, who have not only calmed a mutiny with a word, but have presented themselves single before an army of their enemies; which upon sight of them has revolted from their own leaders, and come over to their trenches. In the rest of Almanzor's actions you see him for the most part victorious; but the same fortune has constantly attended many heroes, who were not imaginary. Yet, you see it no inheritance to him; for, in the first place, he is made a prisoner; and, in the last, defeated, and not able to preserve the city from being taken. If the history of the late Duke of Guise be true, he hazarded more, and performed not less in Naples, than Almanzor is feigned to have done in Granada.

I have been too tedious in this apology; but to make some satisfaction, I will leave the rest of my play exposed to the criticks, without defence.

The concernment of it is wholly passed from me, and ought to be in them who have been favourable to it, and are somewhat obliged to defend their opinions That there are errors in it, I deny not;

Ast opere in tanto fas est obrepere somnum.

But I have already swept the stakes: and, with the common good fortune of prosperous gamesters, can be content to sit quietly; to hear my fortune cursed by some, and my faults arraigned by others; and to suffer both without reply.

John Dryden – A Short Biography

John Dryden was born on August 9th, 1631 in the village rectory of Aldwincle near Thrapston in Northamptonshire, where his maternal grandfather was Rector of All Saints Church.

Dryden was the eldest of fourteen children born to Erasmus Dryden and wife Mary Pickering, paternal grandson of Sir Erasmus Dryden, 1st Baronet (1553–1632) and wife Frances Wilkes, Puritan landowning gentry who supported the Puritan cause and Parliament.

As a boy Dryden lived in the nearby village of Titchmarsh, Northamptonshire where it is probable that he received his first education.

In 1644 he was sent to Westminster School as a King's Scholar where his headmaster was Dr. Richard Busby, a charismatic teacher but severe disciplinarian. Having recently been re-founded by Elizabeth I, Westminster now embraced a very different religious and political spirit encouraging royalism and high Anglicanism but as a humanist public school, it maintained a curriculum which trained pupils in the art of rhetoric and the presentation of arguments for both sides of a given issue. This skill would remain with Dryden and influence his later writing and thinking, as much of it displays these dialectical patterns.

His first published poem, whilst still at Westminster, was an elegy with a strong royalist flavour on the death of his schoolmate Henry, Lord Hastings from smallpox, and alludes to the execution of King Charles I, which took place on January 30th, 1649.

In 1650 Dryden was ready for University and travelled to Trinity College, Cambridge. Dryden's undergraduate years would almost certainly have followed the standard curriculum of classics, rhetoric, and mathematics.

Dryden obtained his BA in 1654, graduating top of the list for Trinity that year.

However family tragedy struck in June of the same year when Dryden's father died, leaving him some land which generated a small income, but not enough to live on.

Returning to London during The Protectorate, Dryden now obtained work with Cromwell's Secretary of State, John Thurloe. This may have been the result of influence exercised on his behalf by his cousin the Lord Chamberlain, Sir Gilbert Pickering.

At Cromwell's funeral on 23 November 1658 Dryden was in the company of the Puritan poets John Milton and Andrew Marvell. The setting was to be a sea change in English history. From Republic to Monarchy and from one set of lauded poets to what would soon become the Age of Dryden.

The start began later that year when Dryden published the first of his great poems, Heroic Stanzas (1658), a eulogy on Cromwell's death which is necessarily cautious and prudent in its emotional display.

With the Restoration of the Monarchy in 1660 Dryden celebrated in verse with Astraea Redux, an authentic royalist panegyric. In this work the interregnum is illustrated as a time of anarchy, and Charles is seen as the restorer of peace and order.

With the king now established Dryden moved quickly to place himself as the leading poet and critic of his day and transferred his allegiances to the new government.

Along with Astraea Redux, Dryden welcomed the new regime with two more panegyrics: To His Sacred Majesty: A Panegyric on his Coronation (1662) and To My Lord Chancellor (1662).

These panegyrics are occasional and written to celebrate events. Thus they are written for the nation rather than the self, but these and others put him in good standing for his eventual appointment as Poet Laureate, where a number of event poems would be required each year and speaking for the Nation and to the Nation would be the first order of duty.

These poems suggest that Dryden was looking to court a possible patron which would have given him an income and time to explore his creative ideas but no, his path instead would be to make a living in writing for publishers, not for the aristocracy, and thus ultimately for the reading public.

In November 1662 Dryden was proposed for membership in the Royal Society, and he was elected an early fellow. However, his inactivity and non payment of dues led to his expulsion in 1666.

On December 1st, 1663 Dryden married the Royalist sister of Sir Robert Howard—Lady Elizabeth Howard (died 1714). The marriage was at St. Swithin's, London, and the consent of the parents is noted on the license, though Lady Elizabeth was then about twenty-five. She was the object of some scandals, well or ill founded; it was said that Dryden had been bullied into the marriage by her brothers. A small estate in Wiltshire was settled upon them by her father. The lady's intellect and temper were apparently not good; her husband was treated as an inferior by those of her social status.

Dryden's works occasionally contain outbursts against the married state but also celebrations of the same. Little else is known of the intimate side of his marriage.

Both Dryden and his wife were warmly attached to their children. They had three sons: Charles (1666–1704), John (1668–1701), and Erasmus Henry (1669–1710). Lady Elizabeth Dryden survived her husband, but went insane soon after his death and died in 1714.

With the re-opening of the theatres after the Puritan ban, Dryden began to also write plays. His first play, The Wild Gallant, appeared in 1663 but was not successful. From 1668 on he was contracted to produce three plays a year for the King's Company, in which he became a shareholder. During the 1660s and '70s, theatrical writing was his main source of income. He led the way in Restoration comedy, his best-known works being Marriage à la Mode (1672), as well as heroic tragedy and regular tragedy, in which his greatest success was All for Love (1678). Dryden was never fully satisfied with his theatrical writings and frequently suggested that his talents were wasted on unworthy audiences.

Certainly therefore fame as a poet looked more rewarding. In 1667, around the same time his dramatic career began, he published Annus Mirabilis, a lengthy historical poem which described the English defeat of the Dutch naval fleet and the Great Fire of London in 1666. It was a modern epic in pentameter quatrains that established him as the pre-eminent poet of his generation, and was crucial in his attaining the posts of Poet Laureate (1668) and then historiographer royal (1670).

When the Great Plague of London closed the theatres in 1665 Dryden retreated to Wiltshire where he wrote Of Dramatick Poesie (1668), arguably the best of his unsystematic prefaces and essays. Dryden constantly defended his own literary practice, and Of Dramatick Poesie, the longest of his critical works, takes the form of a dialogue in which four characters—each based on a prominent contemporary, with Dryden himself as 'Neander'—debate the merits of classical, French and English drama.

He felt strongly about the relation of the poet to tradition and the creative process, and his heroic play Aureng-zebe (1675) has a prologue which denounces the use of rhyme in serious drama. His play All for Love (1678) was written in blank verse, and was to immediately follow Aureng-Zebe.

On December 18th, 1679 he was attacked in Rose Alley near his home in Covent Garden by thugs hired by fellow poet, John Wilmot, 2nd Earl of Rochester, with whom he had a long-standing conflict. Wilmot was constantly in and out of favour with the King and his own poetry was often bawdy, lewd, even obscene and made fun of the King who would often exile him from Court.

Dryden's greatest achievements were in satiric verse: the mock-heroic Mac Flecknoe, a more personal product of his Laureate years, was a lampoon circulated in manuscript and an attack on the playwright Thomas Shadwell. Dryden's main goal in the work is to "satirize Shadwell, ostensibly for his offenses against literature but more immediately we may suppose for his habitual badgering of him on the stage and in print." It is not a belittling form of satire, but rather one which makes his object great in ways which are unexpected, transferring the ridiculous into poetry. This line of satire continued with Absalom and Achitophel (1681) and The Medal (1682). Other major works from this period are the religious poems Religio Laici (1682), written from the position of a member of the Church of England; his 1683 edition of Plutarch's Lives, translated From the Greek by Several Hands in which he introduced the word biography to English readers; and The Hind and the Panther, (1687) which celebrates his conversion to Roman Catholicism.

He wrote Britannia Rediviva celebrating the birth of a son and heir to the Catholic King and Queen on June 10th, 1688. When later in the same year James II was deposed in the Glorious Revolution, Dryden's refusal to take the oaths of allegiance to the new monarchs, William and Mary, which left him out of favour at court and he had to leave his post as Poet Laureate. Thomas Shadwell, his despised rival, succeeded him. Dryden, England's greatest literary figure, was now forced to give up his public offices and live by the proceeds of his pen alone.

Dryden was an excellent translator with his own style which brought the ire of many critics. Many felt he would embellish or expand anything he felt short or curt. Dryden did not feel such expansion was a fault, arguing that as Latin is a naturally concise language it cannot be duly represented by a comparable number of words in the much larger English vocabulary. He continued with his task of translating works by Horace, Juvenal, Ovid, Lucretius, and Theocritus, a task which he found far more satisfying than writing for the stage.

In 1694 he began work on what would be his most ambitious and defining work as translator, The Works of Virgil (1697), which was published by subscription. The publication of the translation of Virgil was a national event and brought Dryden the sum of £1,400.

His final translations appeared in the volume Fables Ancient and Modern (1700), a series of episodes from Homer, Ovid, and Boccaccio, as well as modernised adaptations from Geoffrey Chaucer interspersed with Dryden's own poems. As a translator, he made great literary works in the older languages available to readers of English.

John Dryden died on May 12th, 1700, and was initially buried in St. Anne's cemetery in Soho, before being exhumed and reburied in Westminster Abbey ten days later. He was the subject of poetic eulogies, such as Luctus Brittannici: or the Tears of the British Muses; for the Death of John Dryden, Esq. (London, 1700), and The Nine Muses.

He is seen as dominating the literary life of Restoration England to such a point that the period came to be known in literary circles as the Age of Dryden. Walter Scott called him "Glorious John."

Dryden was the dominant literary figure and influence of his age. He established the heroic couplet as a standard form of English poetry by writing successful satires, religious pieces, fables, epigrams, compliments, prologues, and plays with it; he also introduced the alexandrine and triplet into the form. In his poems, translations, and criticism, he established a poetic diction appropriate to the heroic couplet—Auden referred to him as "the master of the middle style"—that was a model for his contemporaries and for much of the 18th century. The considerable loss felt by the English literary community at his death was evident in the elegies written about him. Dryden's heroic couplet went on to become the dominant poetic form of the 18th century.

What Dryden achieved in his poetry was neither the emotional excitement of the early nineteenth-century romantics nor the intellectual complexities of the metaphysicals. Although he uses formal structures such as heroic couplets, he tried to recreate the natural rhythm of speech, and he knew that different subjects need different kinds of verse. In his preface to Religio Laici he says that "the expressions of a poem designed purely for instruction ought to be plain and natural, yet majestic... The florid, elevated and figurative way is for the passions; for (these) are begotten in the soul by showing the objects out of their true proportion.... A man is to be cheated into passion, but to be reasoned into truth."

Perhaps the following illustrates Dryden and his life—"The way I have taken, is not so streight as Metaphrase, nor so loose as Paraphrase: Some things too I have omitted, and sometimes added of my own. Yet the omissions I hope, are but of Circumstances, and such as wou'd have no grace in English; and the Addition, I also hope, are easily deduc'd from Virgil's Sense. They will seem (at least I have the Vanity to think so), not struck into him, but growing out of him".

Astraea Redux, 1660
The Wild Gallant (comedy), 1663
The Indian Emperour (tragedy), 1665
Annus Mirabilis (poem), 1667
The Enchanted Island (comedy), 1667, with William D'Avenant from Shakespeare's The Tempest
Secret Love, or The Maiden Queen, 1667
An Essay of Dramatick Poesie, 1668
An Evening's Love (comedy), 1668
Tyrannick Love (tragedy), 1669
The Conquest of Granada, 1670
The Assignation, or Love in a Nunnery, 1672
Marriage à la mode, 1672
Amboyna, or the Cruelties of the Dutch to the English Merchants, 1673
The Mistaken Husband (comedy), 1674
Aureng-zebe, 1675
All for Love, 1678
Oedipus (heroic drama), 1679, an adaptation with Nathaniel Lee of Sophocles' Oedipus
Absalom and Achitophel, 1681
The Spanish Fryar, 1681
Mac Flecknoe, 1682
The Medal, 1682
Religio Laici, 1682
To the Memory of Mr. Oldham, 1684
Threnodia Augustalis, 1685
The Hind and the Panther, 1687
A Song for St. Cecilia's Day, 1687
Britannia Rediviva, 1688, written to mark the birth of a Prince of Wales.
Amphitryon, 1690
Don Sebastian (play), 1690
Creator Spirit, by whose aid, 1690. Translation of Rabanus Maurus' Veni Creator Spiritus
King Arthur, 1691
Cleomenes, 1692
The Art of Satire, 1693
Love Triumphant, 1694
The Works of Virgil, 1697
Alexander's Feast, 1697
Fables, Ancient and Modern, 1700

www.ingramcontent.com/pod-product-compliance
Lightning Source LLC
Chambersburg PA
CBHW060131050426
42448CB00010B/2077